Maria P

The Gift of Self

A Spiritual Companion for Separated and Divorced Faithful to the Sacrament of Marriage

Preface by His Excellency Salvatore Di Cristina
Auxiliary Bishop and Vicar General of the
Archdiocese of Palermo

MARY'S ADVOCATES
English

EFFATÁ EDITRICE
Original Italian

Translated and adapted by Peter J. Mango, Ph.D., MLIS

Mary's Advocates' Note:

"The path proposed in this book is adapted only to the case of separated or divorced persons not technically ('morally') responsible for the separation or the divorce" (page 83).

The author quotes the Italian Bishops' Conference "Directory of Family Ministry for the Church in Italy," citing section *Situazioni Particolari* for those separated or divorced. She does not cite section *Eventuali casi di nullità* (Possible cases of nullity).

Famliaris Consortio, in Section 83, describes the ecclesial community's support for those with valid marriages who are separated or divorced. The Code of Canon Law (c. 1151-1155, 1692) is applicable to whoever is not maintaining the common conjugal life.

ISBN 978-0-9965204-0-9

Nihil Obstat: Vincent Gardiner, J.C.L., and Rev. Michael Woost, S.T.L.
Censores Librorum Deputati
March 30, 2016

Imprimatur: Most Rev. Richard G. Lennon, Bishop of Cleveland
May 27, 2016

The *Imprimatur* and *Nihil Obstat* are a declaration that a publication is considered to be free from doctrinal or moral error. It is not implied that those who have granted the *Imprimatur* and *Nihil Obstat* agree with the contents, opinions or statements expressed.

To my husband
And our children,
For the whole Church,
Spouse of Christ,
For the glory of God

In the name of the Father, and of the Son and of the Holy Spirit.

Come Holy Spirit,
Come Spirit of spousal love,
Bear witness
To the merciful love of God

TABLE OF CONTENTS

Preface (Bishop Salvatore Di Cristina) 1
Introduction 3
The Premise 5
Help Along the Way 7

A SPIRITUAL PATH FOR SEPARATED OR DIVORCED SPOUSES FAITHFUL TO THE SACRAMENT

What to Do 11
Separated Spouses and the Parish 12
Flashpoints 16

STAGES IN THE JOURNEY

Separation 22
Rebirth 33
The Desert 39
The Group 46
Reconciliation 53
Renewal of "I Do" 60
The Gift of Self 68
Conclusion 76
Renewal of the "I Do" 78

APPENDIX

Discerning in Specific Situations 82
Testimonies 86
The Spouse is With Us 105
Prayers and Thoughts 111

Recommended Reading 119

Acknowledgements

I wish to thank in a particular way His Excellency the Most Reverend Salvatore Di Cristina, auxiliary bishop and vicar general of the Archdiocese of Palermo, who welcomed this initiative as a special path of conjugal spirituality.

I also wish to thank Monsignor Renzo Bonetti, director of the National Office of Pastoral and Family Life, who with his teachings has helped me make sense of fidelity to the sacrament of marriage.

I likewise wish to thank Don Piero Pasquini of the Caresto Community, who asked that I collaborate in the redaction of the text Un cammino cristiano per i separati ["A Christian Path for Those Separated"] published by Gribaudi (Milan, 2003), from which I have taken points and citations in drafting this current book.

Additionally, I would like to thank Sister Ausilia Bulone, Mother General of the Sisters of Charity of the Prince of Palagonìa, who has welcomed me and other separated persons with affection and compassion, putting at my disposition books and documents of the Servant of God Francesco Voglio Paolo Gravina, the Prince of Palagonía, an exemplary figure for spouses who are separated.

I would be remiss to omit a warm and grateful thought for those priests and deacons who have preserved me within the heart of God, leading me to advance with their counsel, as well, I am certain, with their prayers.

Finally, I wish to thank all those persons, in particular separated persons faithful to the sacrament, who have been of help in the redaction of this work—be it with their counsel, with concrete aid, as well as for respecting the qualities and abilities I thought I had lost on account of my painful story.

PREFACE

This book breathes Easter air.

It is a bit like the house in Bethany where "six days before Passover the sister of Lazarus anointed with a pound of perfumed oil, very precious, the feet of Jesus, *such that the entire house was filled with its fragrance.*"

The ancient Christian commentator Origen asked whether this detail alluded to by the Evangelist was not a mysterious foreshadowing of that fragrance with which Christ inundated the whole great house of God, the Church, through the power of His resurrection three days after His burial.

My impression is this: to follow this book is like experiencing the fragrance of the Crucified One, risen once again. It breathes a serene atmosphere of suffering born with dignity, and of the deep sweetness of one who has tasted both the vinegar of pain and the paternal consolation of God. Yet one becomes aware too of the joy of an even greater forgiveness, of a taste forcefully sweeter than resentment, as well as the joy of fruitful sharing with one's brothers and sisters, rather than morosely withdrawing into solitude.

You can almost touch with your hands the surprising power of faith in the Risen One here: His desire to soothe suffering, to heal wounds, clothed in mercy in the face of any violence suffered. Such is the main message of this book. Its authority flows from the Lord's grace and from experience.

First, though, it has a practical pastoral application.

Dealing with the pastoral situation of Christians married yet separated, and more specifically those who decide to remain faithful to the sacrament of marriage, the author proposes a *spiritual path*. Here the book becomes a right and proper "how to" manual, albeit one that loses none of its ripe spiritual wisdom along the way. This manual is rich in suggestions fed by experience, ranging from a psychological plane to a moral one, to a Spiritual, and even a Liturgical plane.

The book closes with a long appendix in which can be found precious counsels for a pastoral approach toward separated persons; some concrete instances of witness—among which shines the relevant case of Palermo's Servant of God, Francis Paul Gravina, Prince of Palagonìa; as well as an essential collection of prayers and elevations for the spirit suggested by the charming title "The Spouse is With Us," serving as the caption for a beautiful icon of Jesus the Teacher.

One need not claim that this book is proposing an underlying, mature, coherent theology for the phenomenon it treats. Our author-compiler assumes no theological competence. Yet her book is, without doubt, the intuitive fruit of a heart enlightened by faith which has allowed itself to be touched and penetrated by grace. Precisely this is its merit, as noted above, as well as the reason for its authoritativeness.

This book enjoys in every way the privilege of being the "first" text written on the basis of an intuition in this particular matter. This should be recognized above all insofar as it expresses "newness" in the Christian sense of the term, but also insofar as it remains open to being perfected by any further gift of the Spirit.

For all these reasons I wish to accompany this work with my blessing, as well as with my congratulations in the Lord Jesus, the Church's Spouse.

✠ Salvatore Di Cristina
Auxiliary Bishop and Vicar General of the Archdiocese of Palermo

INTRODUCTION

These pages were written by one hand and many hearts, namely those belonging to Gabrielle, Rosy, Paolo, Giancarla, Antoni, and Stephani. And, they were written for all the innocent children of separated persons who are unknown, as are their stories, and for those people whose suffering is so often ignored or not under-stood.

There is a silent Church, one not spoken of much, where these stories of separated spouses that are faithful to the sacrament of marriage make themselves felt as the presence of a something—of Someone—transcending the merely human.

Even though absurd in the eyes of the world, separated persons faithful to the sacrament of matrimony believe that conjugal separation, lived out within the sacrament, "is still a total gift of self, fidelity, and fruitfulness."[1]

It is a total gift of self because it is a gift of themselves offered to the Father, through union with Christ the Spouse, in the Holy Spirit, for the conversion of one's own spouse.

It is fidelity to the conjugal pact made with God, lived out within a chaste continence, sought as a gift, accepted and guarded as such.

---

[1] Catechism of the Catholic Church no.1643.

It is fruitfulness in the Spirit because it is a witness to the fact God remains faithful to His covenant, shared with one's relations and with the world, even when people are idolatrous and unfaithful.

How many times, since Adam and Eve, has humanity broken, through sin, the covenant that God offered?

Still, God does not abandon His creation. He does not create another being and get rid of Adam, nor does He seek out another people to replace Israel.

His love is infinitely merciful.[2]

This must occur in marriage as well, even if one is wounded by separation, when the "first wine" runs out. It is so because the presence of Mary—not to mention of Christ—is not lacking. If this is true, then the Church has the job of helping separated married people who remain faithful to the sacrament of matrimony to travel this path. This is a path which is not the anachronistic imposition of a Church norm received with resigned endurance, but a "path of sanctification lived out within the joyous paradox of the Gospel."[3]

I do not know if, before I die, I will witness the conversion of my husband and my children. But what I am certain of is this—that God loves them more than I do and that He has not forgotten them.

Maria Pia

---

[2] Cf. FC 12.

[3] G. CAMPANELLA, *Ha senso l'indissolubilità del Matrimonio se i due vivono ormai separate?*, in "Presenza," Year IX, n. 5, Parish of San Giuseppe Cottolengo, Palermo, December 1999.

THE PREMISE

> I will give her the vineyards she had, and the valley Achor as a door of hope.
>
> Hos 2:17

A meditation on the Valley of Achor in a passage of the prophet Hosea can be useful for cultivating the theological virtue of hope (Hosea 2:4-25).

Any painful or dramatic situation in our life is transformative and transfiguring *only* if we live it in Christ, with Him, and for Him.

In the Valley of Achor, a family has been shattered. Yet God Himself affirms it is precisely in this place that a ruined family—Hosea's—will find the "portal of hope." A place, in other words, to pass through in order to find yet another one—in the form of a surprising new perspective, a new possibility for life unconsidered till now, since it is divine.

> So God now affirms that the Valley of Achor will no longer mean the tragic end of a family, but instead will become a doorway to hope. A doorway is that thing that permits access to a new place. It is as if God said, 'I place within that situation a possibility of access to a new reality, a new possibility of life. It will become a portal of hope…' It is important to emphasize that God *and He alone* is in a position to transform precisely that place into a *portal of hope—the Valley of Achor.* It is not a different situation, but precisely the same one which becomes a *portal of hope.*
>
> One day the Lord told Jeremiah to go down to the potter's shop (cf. Jeremiah 18:1-4). Jeremiah went and watched a potter working the clay with a potter's wheel. The prophet noted that

if a jar broke, the potter took the clay in hand and began again remaking that jar with the same mud, without changing the material. This episode from Jeremiah's life contains a precious spiritual pointer: in our case the Lord does not change the material, but first begins from where we are, from what we are, from our attributes and our limitations, and from this He recon-structs within us a new possibility of life.

This is the God of the Bible. This is good and beautiful news for every couple that is living through moments of difficulty (as it is for every separated person remaining faithful to the sacrament). They need not become other than what they are already, and in this way allow God's love to act.[4]

---

[4] G. VIVADELLI, *Immagini della coppia nella Bibbia*, San Paolo, Milano, 2003, pp.41-62.

HELP ALONG THE WAY

For the separated person who wishes to follow the course proposed here, it is without a doubt more beneficial to examine excerpts from "Stages in the Journey," (page 20) praying and meditating on one of the passages suggested or else on other passages from the Gospel.

One should proceed without haste. Within a group setting, this path provides about a year's worth of material. Walking together with a group facilitates the path toward the gift of self.

The separated person who follows this path, alone or in a group, may repeat the various stages as needed.

The following may be organized:

- To facilitate the path to forgiveness, beyond meditating on the Gospel passages adopted, one can organize a prayer meeting in which to ask the Lord for the grace to be able to forgive;
- For the renewal of marital consent, having first understood the premise, it is helpful to do a weekend retreat, appreciating that wedding reception of the Lamb of God to which all the baptized are called.

For the Saturday evening on such a retreat, it is important to perform Eucharistic adoration using texts that reflect Christ's spousal side.

Regarding the "Prayer for the Marriage Vows Renewal" (page 78), it is good to have married couples, director of pastoral work, and even engaged couples participate. All present will experience a moment of great grace.

A SPIRITUAL PATH FOR SEPARATED OR DIVORCED FAITHFUL TO THE SACRAMENT

WHAT TO DO

Conjugal separation, lived out in Christ by the grace of the sacrament of matrimony, can be an occasion of sanctification for the spouse who has been abandoned, the spouse who left, and for the children.

For the deserted spouse who does not intend to follow alternate routes proposed by the world to annul the suffering of abandonment and fill a void for affection, one of two attitudes may be adopted:

- To remain alone believing erroneously, that this is merely a norm willed by the Church;
- To continue to live out sacramental matrimony as a vocation, continuing each day to choose their marriage right to the end.

The Christian community and pastoral family workers often feel unprepared to serve separated people.

In fact, various attitudes might be adopted on their part: fear of doing damage due to a lack of preparation in addressing such suffering; the prejudicial belief that separated people, will sooner or later end up seeking easier solutions proposed by the world anyway even at times of a certain indifference to the grave problem of conjugal separation; and, finally, some believe that if the separated person has chosen to remain alone, then everything has been resolved, so there is no need to help.

As a matter of fact, the separated person who did not wish for separation is more often than not experiencing an anguished and critical moment in his or her life.

Often even the closest family members are incapable of helping in an effective way due to their own emotional involvement, and they are unable to manage being a real comfort to the separated.

SEPARATED SPOUSES AND THE PARISH

Separated persons seek support on the part of the parish community. This support, in addition to being welcoming, can be a human comfort and an aid to reinforcing their faith.

Some separated persons draw close to the Church in search of the meaning of suffering. These people are more open and available to begin a spiritual path. They desire to bear witness to the fact that separation can be borne with dignity, raising the children and seek-ing to keep the family united, albeit while experiencing great wounds as a spouse and parent. That is why it is indispensable to have a reference point, especially at the beginning of the separation when the person being left feels disoriented.

Others by the grace of God, and aided by the community, can come to forgive as Jesus asks us, since one's spouse—even if he or she has every fault in the book—is still forever created in the image of God.

At this point the spouse faithful to the sacrament, who after a spiritual path arrives to the summit of the meaning of suffering, can contemplate from there God's own horizon, the actual mission of sacramental marriage. *This other person joined to me, indissolubly, remains entrusted to me by God Himself, such that I must intercede for his or her conversion and salvation.*

The parish then has the delicate task of welcoming the separated person, and of proposing a spiritual path adapted to his or her situation. Consequently, an attentive discernment is needed to distinguish particular situations.

Welcome

Here are some suggestions:

> The first meeting with a person who approaches the parish looking for help with family difficulties is fundamental. This is the time for *being a neighbor*, for bearing the burden of others' sufferings, for offering a sign of hope. If the one seeking help from the parish receives no immediate response to these needs, it is most likely he or she will turn to paths that distance him or her from Christ, for example, seeking a new romantic relationship, having recourse to occult practices, or even committing extreme acts out of desperation.
>
> The task, then, of the parish is to create a welcoming climate, listening and seeking to establish a trustful rapport. Whoever comes seeking help from the Church must find something tangible—as tangible as the mire Christ placed in eyes of the blind man to heal him.[5]

Possible Aids

The first thing is to offer a word of consolation, expressing sentiments of empathy and esteem. In fact in the *Directory of Family Ministry for the Church in Italy*, we read:

> The Christian community, beginning with priests, and couples composed of judicious spouses, should draw near to others considerately, discretely, and in a spirit of solidarity:
>
> - Recognizing above all the value of the witness to fidelity borne by an innocent spouse, accepting the suffering and loneliness this new situation entails;
> - Granting them esteem, understanding, heartfelt solidarity and concrete help;

---

[5] COMMUNITA DI CARESTO, *Un cammino cristiano per i separati*, Gribaudi, Milano 2003, p.95.

- Recognizing that their situation in life does not preclude them from admission to the sacraments. In its own way, in fact, the condition of separation at this point remains a proclamation of the value of the indissolubility of marriage.[6]

Nor should it be forgotten that, "the person's needs, different from one case to the next, may be:"

- Material: finding a place to live, gainful employment, or meeting the children's physical needs;
- Emotional: expressing feelings of esteem, empathy, or meeting the children's emotional needs;
- Spiritual: discovering a personal path; meeting the children's needs for spiritual growth.[7]

The parish can be a true, concrete help and reference point for all those persons who so often have faced a family crisis alone or with merely human instruments and strategies.

In this way the parish offers what the world lacks: Christ. To us, who bear His name, is entrusted the task of revealing Him through the love we bear toward our brothers and sisters, especially if they are weakened or suffering.

---

[6] ITALIAN EPISCOPAL CONFERENCE, *Direttorio di Pastorale Familiare per la Chiesa in Italia* (Directory of Family Ministry for the Church in Italy), Mediagraf 1993, Chapter Seven. nos. 208-209.

(English Publisher's note) Before the introduction in the *Direttorio di pastorale familiare per la Chiesa in Italia*, there is included *La Papola Del Papa* (The word of the Pope). Pope John Paul II explained the significance and importance of the *Directory of Family Ministry for the Church in Italy*. Full text available at www.chiesacattolica.it.

[7] COMMUNITA DI CARESTO, *Un cammino cristiano per i separati*, p.102.

Spiritual Accompaniment

If the parish creates a climate of fraternal charity, offering attention and concrete help and compensating for the person's emotional void, it doubtless will be able to lend support and spiritual aid when accompanying a brother or sister to gradual inner healing. It will also help him or her live out the mission of sacramental marriage in accordance with God's plan. Just as important, this climate of fraternal charity can lead not only one's own sanctification, but also to that of the spouse entrusted to one by God.

Spiritual accompaniment has as its final goal the rediscovery of sacramental marriage and its mission of reinforcing faith, reviving hope, and activating charity.[8]

---

[8] Cf. *ibidem*, p.96.

FLASHPOINTS

Infidelity (Adultery)

Here are some motivational thoughts for separated persons:

- It is so beautiful to see you remaining faithful to the sacrament, even if just for today.
- Offer this to God as your daily decision, and He will reward you for it.
- Remember that no one knows anything about the future. We do not know where we will be ten years down the line or even an hour from now. It is a mistake, above all for those who separated, to peer too far into the future. The future too is God's gift.
- Reflect on the fact that not even couples who are still together can be certain of the fidelity of each of their spouses (in the future).
- The same holds true for priests.
- Remember that since fidelity is God's gift, one must ask for it day after day.

One can find oneself in the unforeseen situation of the absence of conjugal relations. After years of living together one faces a situation that had never been considered seriously before.

Yet even couples must live out that chastity which is proper to couples. Who—say if a spouse is in the hospital with a coma—

considers him or herself compelled to engage in sex, and for this reason exonerates him or herself from marital fidelity?

We who are separated have a spouse who *is* in an extremely grave coma: a spiritual coma. If it is difficult to maintain oneself in chaste continence, this once again is a chance to ask God for the gift of this virtue. The same virtue is asked of every Christian who wishes to be a disciple of Jesus. He was poor, chaste, and obedient.

In contrast to what certain pseudo-scientists would have us believe, the human person can, by a free and conscious choice, refrain from exercising genital sexuality without becoming a repressed and incomplete individual.

A key point is to distinguish between men and women, and between younger and older people. For the first category—especially when young and male—the world is convinced it is not possible to live in chastity. Advice is often offered in counseling or psychological publications on how to choose the "next" partner. It is important to build a defensive barrier around weaker or more disoriented brothers who are in danger of collapsing into self-destruction in this area.

Paradoxically, at a time in history when chastity is no longer seen as a human value, we faithful separated spouses become witnessses to what the world claims is impossible. Everything is possible to the one who entrusts himself or herself to God.

"Widow" / "Widower"

Since in our case, no one dies, I reject these terms as suggesting a baleful end to everything. Ours is not a religion of death. We are disciples of the risen Christ.

The two disciples of Emmaus also "walked with long faces, arguing with each other," (cf. Luke 24:13-35). The world often says, "Now there is nothing more to do but face facts." Yet can it be that everything is over, and that our eyes are unable to see? In this same passage the Lord Himself draws near to them—and to us—asking, as if surprised, "What are you *saying*...?" To Mary Magdalene, too, who wept before Christ's empty tomb (cf. John 20:11-18), Jesus asks a seemingly incredible question, "Woman, why are you weeping? Who are you looking for?"

It is important to cultivate the theological virtue of hope, and the Mother of God helps us in this. Mary renewed her "I do" to God at the foot of the cross, expecting, in the silence of Holy Saturday, that God's work would be revealed to her and to all humanity.

"Broken Family"

It would be more apt and charitable to say "wounded family," and not give children the idea they are somehow bereft of hope. What is more, "all things work for the good for those who love God," (Romans 8:28), so there is no situation which cannot be transfigured by His mysterious love when presented to Him with humility and a contrite heart.

"Ex"

It is common to say "ex-husband," "ex-wife," or "ex-spouse." This gives the impression of a relationship which has ceased altogether—something which is impossible within the bounds of the sacrament of matrimony.

"Single" / "Single Again"

The separated or divorced person cannot be considered single because he or she is always espoused in virtue of the indissolubility of marriage. The phrase "single again" is inapplicable because it implies that one is therefore free to search for the next partner.

"Maybe this was not the right person"

Just what is this supposed to mean? That the separation occurred because there was a mistake in selection? But is this true? Or does God have a plan which—in this situation—is yet to be revealed?

"Since I was the one abandoned, I can seek a new companion"

This seems like a pretty thin consolation prize; just a patch on torn clothing. "No one puts a piece of new material on an old garment, because the patch bursts and the tear gets worse," (Matthew 9:16).

Even in the periodic cases of the declaration of nullity, there is always a personal wound to heal, and forgiveness to offer.

STAGES IN THE JOURNEY

Deep waters cannot quench love,
nor floods sweep it away.

Songs of Songs, 8:7

SEPARATION

My eyes are dimmed
with sorrow.

Psalm 6:8

Goal of the Stage

To rebuild yourself, valued as a unique being; willed, created and loved by God.

To bring yourself to an awareness of the great dignity of being a child of God.

Description of the path

That which we have sought to avoid in every way—conjugal separation—sadly is what we now confront.

It is as if a tornado of unspeakable violence has whirled round us. We feel disoriented, stunned, and empty of all energy. We often live at half our capacity, unable to draw up further plans for our life. It is hard to sleep at night, and the morning seems like a waking nightmare. The painful reality hits our mind with all its brute force:

> An indescribable and unimaginable pain takes hold of us. If, as the Lord says, *'the two will become one flesh,'* then separation is like tearing apart a living body.[9]

The suffering is so unsustainable it can even lead to gestures of extreme violence toward oneself or one's own family members, as we sadly learn from the daily news.

"It is the darkest moment of our married experience!"[10]

Yet it is also the moment in which Christ approaches to ask us, "Will you leave too?" (John 6:67).

We prefer to decline what seems so horrible to us—the cross. In the end we may accept it, thinking we are surrendering ourselves to an instrument of torture willed by God; yet we will discover that, on the contrary, we've surrendered to His love. Because it is only by accepting the cross that we can find what we were seeking: Him, His love.

During the first days of separation we are immersed in, and overwhelmed by, a sea of emotions:

† Fear of losing our children's affection;

† Guilt and shame at not having been able to avoid the division;

† Rage against everything and everyone;

† Contempt for, and hostility toward, a spouse who does not care about the wounds he or she is causing

† Disbelief over what has happened;

† Dismay;

† Disorientation and an inability to undertake any plans whatsoever;

† Aversion to the other sex.

---

[9] COMMUNITA DI CARESTO, *Un cammino cristiano per i separati*, Gribaudi, Milano 2003, p.30.

[10] *Ibidem*.

Moreover, we must mention such forms of extreme pathology such as panic attacks, phobias, apathy, grave depression, etc. We feel as if we are on quicksand, without fixed points of reference. We trust no one, not even ourselves. Confronted with the collapse of our marriage we ask ourselves, "Where did I go wrong?" It is a question that will hammer at us for a long time, hollowing out an abyss inside of us. "Where…? What might I have done…? Why…?" We ransack our memory for the story all over again, but without finding answers to our questions. Everything we ever did for our spouse and our family now seems meaningless, irretrievably lost. We see only a pile of rubble from which to dig out the hope of finding something salvageable. Now and then, thinking we have found something of value worth saving, we turn to pray in pain:

> Lord, there was this plan to grow old together, raise our children to adulthood with attention and care. But You, Lord, shaking your head, took those things that continued to hurt us from our hands, tenderly whispering to us, 'It is too little…Too little. Look at *me*.'
>
> Now, in silence, there remains nothing else but to contemplate You crucified, as this prayer spontaneously wells up within us:
>
> Even You, Lord, nailed to the cross,
> Seemed to have failed in everything:
> You came to announce the Kingdom of God and speak of the Father,
> But no one believed You,
> Nor recognized You as God's Son;
> You passed by, blessing,
> Healing the sick and paralytics,
> Casting out demons,
> Raising the dead,
> Blessing and feeding the crowds…
> Yet in Your moment of trial,
> No one testified on Your behalf.

After a night spent in prayer, You chose the twelve disciples,
Teaching them as You lived with them for three years,
Calling them friends and loving them to the end.
Yet where were they in Your time of trial,
Of condemnation, scourging and crucifixion?
Of twelve, only one, John,
Had the courage to be near You up to Your death on the cross.
The others: the greater part fled;
Judas betrayed You and sold You;
While Peter denied You three times.
Still You, Lord, continued to love them.
Contemplating You on the cross,
I feel the storms of my heart quieted.
You alone command the unruly blasts of my heart to cease,
The floods of my heart to be at peace.
From this contemplation of You,
Innocent Crucified One,
I receive what You alone can give.
The peace of the Risen One who enters locked doors
and says, "*Shalom!* Peace be with you."

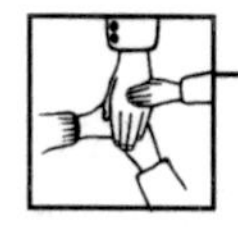

Possible Aids

To give you an idea of the situation, I am reminded of one of those newscasts that shows a nighttime scene of collapsed walls and the ruins of a home destroyed by the effects of an earthquake. It is nighttime. There is no light. The walls have collapsed. Family intimacy is gone. Whoever passes by shakes his head, and looters are quick to take advantage of the situation.[11]

'Looters' are those who approach a separated person to exploit his or her disorientation. They are false consolers.

---

11 *Un cammino cristiano per i separati*, cit., p.31.

In fact, they are people inspired by personal interests of various kinds: financial, sexual, the desire to have power over another person by rendering him or her dependent, etc.

To keep this from happening the Christian community should show a personal interest, building a defensive "barrier" around those sheep which are most vulnerable and exposed:

> In this phase the *fraternal and tactful presence of a priest*, as well as that of a stable couple with the patience to bear with a lot of lamentation. The priest and couple are needed to dry those desperate tears and help re-create a family atmosphere for the wounded person, as well as for the children.[12]

What is required is a lot of listening, fewer exhortations, and more words of consolation accompanied by words of *practical* help.

Every intervention should have as its objective reminding the separated person of his or her dignity as a child of God, who is desired and loved, unique and irreplaceable; and who is a person created in His image and likeness, called to be a protagonist in God's plan.

To concrete manifestations of help must be added a path for growth in faith and hope. This must be done in a gradual way, taking into account the kind of spiritual formation the person has received, and taking baby steps, especially in the first few months.

Personal prayer is important because it comforts and strengthens. Yet while it certainly is the first resource to take advantage of, it is not enough to empower our faith. Lingering solely in the sphere of prayer, one can fall into devotionalism, which does not help one to grow.

---

12 Ibidem.

Today more than ever the Christian must be prepared to offer a reason for his or her faith.

> Dear families, you too should be fearless, ever ready to give witness to the hope that is in you (cf. 1 Peter 3:15), since the Good Shepherd has put that hope in your hearts through the Gospel…Do not be afraid of the risks![13]

To give witness, a solid Christian formation in the sacrament of marriage founded upon God's Word and upon the Church's magis-terial teachings is required.

It is necessary to develop the daily habit of reading God's Word. If one attentively contemplates on the verses, a little reading may be enough.

For a variety of reasons, an excellent habit is to read the Gospel of that day's Mass. First, personal participation in the Eucharistic celebration can become increasingly more conscious. Second, it follows the pedagogical path of the Liturgical Years A, B, and C; and, last but not least, it broadens and deepens one's knowledge of God's Word.

Daily Mass is a moment of great grace and help on a path of spiritual growth, above all in times of suffering. One can attend weekday Mass before work in the morning, at noon, or in the evening. If this really is impossible, one can at least make a visit to Jesus in the Eucharist for a few minutes.

Of course, suggestions should be made to the separated person taking into account their education, sensitivities, and degree of openness. "The task of a companion along the way might not be that of offering solutions, but of helping a separated person walk on his or her own, equipping them."[14] Such a companion can target the most effective strategies, so the

---

[13] *Letter to Families from Pope John Paul II*, No.18.

[14] *Un cammino cristiano per i separati*, cit., p.31.

separated person can gradually overcome those emotional, theoretical, and external obsta-cles in the way of unleashing one's full potential in the areas of body, psyche, and spirit. In the first phases of accompaniment one should be like one of those companions of the paralyzed man who were willing to climb the roof and remove tiles in order to get him to Jesus (Mark 2:3-12).

> One must take care regarding the separated person's humanly hoping to witness the return of a spouse. There is the danger that a separated person will embrace prayer as if it were a magical act for the purpose of turning everything to the way it was before! When the time is right, it should be made clear tactfully that, while leaving open the possibility of a spouse's eventual return, what is needed is to cultivate the theological virtue of hope rather than illusions that lead to a roadblock, if not to despair.[15]

How long this may last no one can say, since so much depends on the recipient's degree of spiritual maturity. What is critical is that one's companions on the way create a welcoming atmosphere, one in which the separated person does not feel judged for whatever personal mistakes he or she may have made. The presence of an-other separated person of the same gender could also be important, although perhaps not right away, given that the idea of not being able to reestablish the couple-relationship is initially rejected.

As noted before, in addition to spiritual support must be added concrete solidarity regarding the real demands of both the separated person and the children. Often mothers must leave the child-ren to work outside the home for several hours to support the family. One can help with doctors' visits, taking kids to CCD, the weekly expenses, offering car rides in general, etc.

---

[15] Ibidem, p.38.

If there are no grandparents or parents close by who can help, one should be prompt to offer gestures of solidarity, as with any true family. In a certain sense, the separated person and his or her children should be "adopted" by the parish community.

One concept to remember is that of speaking with the separated person's family of origin: brothers, sisters, or parents. These are people who, even if indirectly, suffer from this situation too. It is appropriate to support them emotionally as well as spiritually. One should seek, simultaneously, to elicit from within the family of origin whatever concrete help may be needed.

Mistakes to Avoid

- Avoid encouraging a separated person to volunteer for work in which he or she encounters other situations of suffering, like that of cancer patients. A separated person might feel worse, rather than better!
- Do not underestimate the mistake of offering the separated person time-consuming tasks within the parish that distract from the mission of the sacrament of marriage.

Personal Reflections

Suffering is bound up with human life.

- Can I avoid it? How should I confront it?
- How did Jesus and Mary live out their suffering?

Here are some readings for meditation:

From Psalm 55: 2-4, 13-15, 17-20

Listen, God, to my prayer;
do not hide from my pleading;
hear me and give answer.
I rock with grief; I groan
at the uproar of the enemy,
the clamor of the wicked.
They heap trouble upon me,
savagely accuse me." [...]
"For it is not an enemy that reviled me –
that I could bear –
Not a foe who viewed me with contempt,
from that I could hide.
But it was you, my other self,
my comrade and friend,
You, whose company I enjoyed,
at whose side I walked
in the house of God." [...]
"But I will call upon God,
and the LORD will save me.
At dusk, dawn, and noon
I will grieve and complain,
and my prayer will be heard.
He will redeem my soul in peace
from those who war against me,
though there are many who oppose me.
God, who sits enthroned forever,
will hear me and afflict them.

Mark 4:36-41

Leaving the crowd, they took Him with them in the boat just as he was, and other boats were with Him. A violent squall came up and waves were breaking over the boat, so that it was already filling up. Jesus was in the stern, asleep on a cushion. They woke Him and said to Him, "Teacher, do You not care that we are perishing?" He woke up, rebuked the wind, and said to the sea, "Quiet! Be still!" The wind ceased and there was great calm. Then He asked them, "Why are you terrified? Do you not yet have faith?" They were filled with great awe and said to one another, "Who then is this whom even wind and sea obey?"

Matthew 16:24-25

Then Jesus said to His disciples, "Whoever wishes to come after Me must deny himself, take up his cross, and follow Me. For whoever wishes to save his life will lose it, but whoever loses his life for My sake will find it."

From the Apostolic Letter *Salvifici Doloris* of the Supreme Pontiff John Paul II

9. Within each form of suffering endured by man, and at the same time at the basis of the whole world of suffering, there inevitably arises *the question: why*? It is a question about the cause, the reason, and equally, about the purpose of suffering, and, in brief, a question about its meaning. Not only does it accompany human suffering, but it seems even to determine its human content, what makes suffering precisely human suffering.

It is obvious that pain, especially physical pain, is widespread in the animal world. But only the suffering human being knows that he is suffering and wonders why; and he suffers in a humanly speaking still deeper way if he does not find a satisfactory answer. This is a *difficult question*, just as is a question closely akin to it, the question of evil. Why does evil exist? Why is there evil in the world? When we put the question in this way, we are always, at least to a certain extent, asking a question about suffering too.

Both questions are difficult, when an individual puts them to another individual, when people put them to other people, as also when man *puts them to God*. For man does not put this question to the world, even though it is from the world that suffering often comes to him, but he puts it to God as the Creator and Lord of the world. And it is well known that concerning this question there not only arise many frustrations and conflicts in the relations of man with God, but it also happens that people reach the point of actually *denying God.* For, whereas the existence of the world opens as it were the eyes of the human soul to the existence of God, to His wisdom, power and greatness, evil and suffering seem to obscure this image, sometimes in a radical way, especially in the daily drama of so many cases of undeserved suffering and of so many faults without proper punishment. So this circumstance shows—perhaps more than any other—the importance of *the question of the meaning of suffering*; it also shows how much care must be taken both in dealing with the question itself and with all possible answers to it.

13. But in order to perceive the true answer to the "why" of suffering, we must look to the revelation of divine love, the ultimate source of the meaning of everything that exists. Love is also the richest source of the meaning of suffering, which always remains a mystery. We are conscious of the insufficiency and inadequacy of our explanations. Christ causes us to enter into the mystery and to discover the "why" of suffering, as far as we are capable of grasping the sublimity of divine love.

In order to discover the profound meaning of suffering, following the revealed word of God, we must open ourselves wide to the human subject in his manifold potentiality. We must above all accept the light of Revelation not only insofar as it expresses the transcendent order of justice but also insofar as it illuminates this order with Love, as the definitive source of everything that exists. Love is also the fullest source of the answer to the question of the meaning of suffering. This answer has been given by God to man in the cross of Jesus Christ.

REBIRTH

Your word is a lamp for my feet,
a light for my path.

Psalm 119:105

Goal of the Stage

Entrust yourself to God. Strengthen your faith.

Description of the path

The first steps

Accept the cross and ask God for help.

"It is time for the meeting. It is truly as Lord that God enters our life, but only if we wish and permit it."[16]

"Behold, I stand at the door and knock. If anyone hears My voice and opens the door, I will enter his house and dine with him, and he with Me" (Revelation 3:20).

How many times has the Lord knocked at the door of our life? Yet, perhaps thinking we were not yet ready to receive Him, we left Him outside. Or maybe we only let Him into the guest room, or into the parlor—as if He were a stranger. Yet we have not

[16] *Un cammino cristiano per i separati*, cit., p.36.

given Him permission to enter into the most intimate room of our heart.

Yet He is our friend, He comes to help us, offering us His love. "God loves us to the point of leaving us free to reject His Love."[17] He offers Himself as the Eternal Lover; and it is only if we offer our consent freely and voluntarily that there can be a valid union.

Throughout Sacred Scripture. the love of God is presented as a spousal covenant, because a marriage is valid only if there is consent freely given by both parties. Thus, the love of God is such that it respects our freedom. He leaves us free even when we make mistakes or even betray Him, while offering us a chance at repentance. "And you taught your people, by these deeds, that those who are just must be kind; And you gave your sons good ground for hope that you would permit repentance for their sins," (Wisdom 12:19). "He alone is capable of enduring more patiently (*patior*) for us to accept His gift of Love: Jesus Christ."[18]

We, unfortunately, live with a fear of this encounter. (cf. Genesis 3:10), assuming it may upset and trample our entire life. We do not know who it is we are resisting. "Jesus answered and said… 'If you knew the gift of God and who is saying to you, 'Give Me a drink,' you would have asked Him and He would have given you living water,'" (John 4:10).

> Yet we know from the Gospels that it is by means of the narrow road and the cross that we are able to achieve that fullness of life which leads us to Christ. Our resisting only hinders the Easter event of our life. Yet *now* is the moment to surrender totally to God. Now is the moment to *entrust* ourselves fully to His work, now is the moment to *allow* Him to love us in full freedom.[19]

---

[17] Ibidem.

[18] Ibidem.

[19] Ibidem, p.37.

The "mustard seed" sown in our heart at baptism begins to germinate when watered by a simple prayer of abandonment, by a "yes" renewed every day, and in all situations.

Spiritual growth is nourished above all by three daily moments dedicated to our encounter with the Lord:

- Eucharistic communion during the celebration of Holy Mass;
- Reading and meditating on God's Word;
- Personal prayer.

Prayer, at the beginning, can be brief but should be frequent throughout the day; like seeds which are watered little but often, allowing tender sprouts to absorb just that amount of water that will help them grow and develop, without danger of drying up or wilting. Day after day, silently but gradually, faith grows, growing ever deeper and more robust roots capable of offering support against those things which tend to uproot it.

We have got to reinforce ourselves for spiritual combat. The best nourishment, after the Eucharist and prayer, is meditating on God's Word every day. Even just one verse is enough for the week, if it is well reflected upon. To get results it may be useful to change something about our daily habits. For example if one is not habituated to morning prayer, it may be enough to get up a little earlier than we are used to and encounter the Lord. He is already waiting to welcome us for the first "appointment" of the day.

Prayer is a time for secrets of the heart, for telling God everything: what we want, what is hurting us, in simple and direct language. Out of this first morning encounter we derive strength to dedicate ourselves to the demands of the day.

It is good to have frequent recourse to God throughout the day. A cry from the heart causes God's hand to descend quickly upon us, to swoop us up precisely when we feel crushed by suffering. Other times of intimacy can be created in the early afternoon and evening. A few minutes are sufficient at first.

A very important, even precious, opportunity for personal prayer may be found during the hours of the night. If during the night we are awake or even suffer from insomnia, we can dedicate this time to prayer. We can have recourse to God's Mother, who is always prompt to help us, as any true mother would. Simply meditating using the Rosary, asking the holy Virgin Mary to accompany us, allows us to promptly experience her loving care for us.

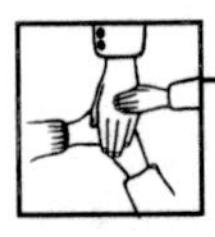

Possible Aids

- It is preferable that only one priest follow the spiritual growth of the separated person: first, to avoid that—in switching from one priest to another—the person winds up having to recount his or her story all over again, thereby reliving the suffering caused by still-recent events. In addition, if the spiritual guide remains the same, he will be in a position to gradually introduce this person to various ways of praying, offering readings or some words of comfort, or exhortation according to the needs of the moment.
- If the separated person can spare the time, he or she might be offered light responsibilities to help them recognize themselves as belonging to that family of families the parish is supposed to be. For example, he or she can read during the Eucharistic celebration; thanks to this he or she can be formed in the meditative reading of God's Word. What is more, such a reader does not just read a communication aloud, he or she *proclaims* the Word. This responsibility can offer an opportunity for the person to meditate on the readings for the following Sunday throughout the week. He or she should realize that a Sunday reader must proclaim with a pure heart, and thus one should seek out this virtue, asking God for it.

Personal Reflections

- In Gethsemane Jesus prayed while in a state of anguish (cf. Luke 22:39-46). Am I willing to accompany Him through meditation, contemplation, and the adoration of His suffering?
- Do I have recourse to prayer every time I feel deluged by pain, loneliness, and anguish?
- Do I ask God to strengthen my faith, so that I can abandon myself totally to His wise and loving will?

Here are some readings for meditation:

Luke 22:39-46

> Then going out He went, as was his custom, to the Mount of Olives, and the disciples followed him. When He arrived at the place He said to them, "Pray that you may not undergo the test." After withdrawing about a stone's throw from them and kneeling, He prayed, saying, "Father, if You are willing, take this cup away from Me; still, not My will but Yours be done." (And to strengthen Him an angel from heaven appeared to Him. He was in such agony and He prayed so fervently that His sweat became like drops of blood falling on the ground.) When He rose from prayer and returned to His disciples, He found them sleeping from grief. He said to them, "Why are you sleeping? Get up and pray that you may not undergo the test."

Mathew 21:22

> "Whatever you ask for in prayer with faith, you will receive."

Mark 5:35-36

> While He was still speaking, people from the synagogue official's house arrived and said, "Your daughter has died; why trouble the teacher any longer?" Disregarding the message that was reported, Jesus said to the synagogue official, "Do not be afraid; just have faith."

THE DESERT

I will betroth you to me with fidelity,
and you shall know the LORD.

Hosea 2:22

Goal of the Stage

To cultivate a personal and intimate relationship with God.

Description of the path

It can happen, albeit less nowadays, that a desert forms around separated persons.

At first friends may call to invite them to life as it was before: one's "normal" output level, one's "usual" plans. But the separated person often feels like a fish out of water, ill at ease, because he or she fails to find the consolation needed in the present moment. Often he or she is encouraged to "hit reset" or find another partner. Some shake their heads at the decision we have made, and this is of no help to us.

It is rare to find someone who decides to set aside the time, a heart listening to our heart so deeply wounded and torn. Little by little, one finds oneself in a desert, that had been unknown to us up till then, making it all the more empty and agonizing.

Yet it is here that the Lord leads us for a truly intimate and personal talk, to speak "heart to heart."[20]

The dramatic desert produced in crucifixion is transformed by the Spirit into that arid desert of which Hosea speaks (cf. Hosea 2:5). The desert becomes a place of intimacy. The Spirit leads Christ and His Spouse into the desert so they can talk heart to heart. Of this intimate conversation, He is both the agent and champion.

This encounter turns into an intimate understanding and a delirious joy.

Thus, the moment of death and of abandonment becomes a moment of conjugal intimacy. "So I will allure her; I will lead her into the desert and speak to her heart ...She shall respond there as in the days of her youth," (Hosea 2:16-17b).[21]

It is the moment in which the God who is Love wishes to leave with His beloved. And so, not to be disturbed, He looks for an out-of-the-way place. The Lord declares His love, the fact that He wishes to espouse Himself to us (cf. Hosea 2:21-22).

The Lord seduces us with His patience, offering us His love. He does not ask for His love to be returned, but simply that one accepts His healing and saving love: *"Take and eat...take and drink..."*

During the Eucharistic celebration the Lord bends over our wounds like a physician, healing and binding them up. In confession He peels off soiled bandages, curing the heart's wounds by pouring over them the oil of consolation (His Word) and the wine of hope (the Eucharist), bandaging them anew with His love. Only in this way can one return home to confront the day-to-day alone. Yet a certain serenity and peace already begins to reveal itself. Though the situation has not changed, *we* are changed by *accepting the Lord's loving care.* Now

[20] *Un cammino cristiano per i separati*, cit., p.42.

[21] G. MAZZANTI, *Mistero pasquale mistero nuziale*, EDB, Bologna 2002, p.43.

the solitude is not so terrifying, because we begin to experience His comforting presence.

Our spouse has left us with those hollow spaces that may never be filled by another person, or a new activity. They are spaces God alone can fill, which He alone can pass through in a healing way.[22]

As one regains spiritual energies, a purification phase begins. In fact, gradually we are able to bear the weight, and the Lord progressively reveals our errors in the light of His Word. Jesus approaches to purify us, to cleanse us.

Christ the Spouse who has:

loved the Church and handed Himself over for her to sanctify her, cleansing her by the bath of water with the word, that he might present to Himself the Church in splendor, without spot or wrinkle or any such thing, that she might be holy and without blemish, (Ephesians 5:25-27).

It is a journey to be made with prudence, and without being forced, because when one becomes aware of one's own errors and their consequences, there is a risk of falling into anguish and despair.

Limited by human possibility, irreparable events may occur; but they can be transfigured by God when we hand them over to Him. God alone is the master of time, and the prayers of today can heal the wounds of the past. God can allow to emerge within our consciousness any mistakes which have been committed.

A companion along the way may, opportunely, highlight that merciful love God has for everyone. God does not reject the sinner, but on the contrary seeks him or her out. "Jesus heard this

---

[22] *Un cammino cristiano per i separati*, cit., p.43.

and said to them, 'Those who are well do not need a physician, but the sick do. I did not come to call the righteous but sinners.'"

Chapter 15 of Luke's Gospel gives us the parables of the Lost Sheep, of the Lost Coin, and the return of the Prodigal Son, wherein Jesus underscores the joy produced by one sinner's repentance—to the point of His throwing a party. "'Because your brother was dead and has come to life again; he was lost and has been found,'" (Luke 15:32).

If the person feels guilty, one can point out that we have all had lapses—not so as to render these events merely banal, but to lighten the weight flowing from cognizance that one has shared in many wounds, received and given.

Often what we have committed are the fruit of familiar habits considered "normal," or based on the wrong idea about what is acceptable. In this phase what ought to be born in our heart is a true contrition that will urge us to no longer commit certain missteps and sins, having recourse to the indispensable and irreplaceable help of God's grace. A sentiment of expiation wells up within us, not as a time for punishment, but as a path of purification (from the Greek *piur* = fire), immersed in the fire of the Holy Spirit.

It is necessary to grow in humility to accept God's merciful love. Recognizing the poor quality of our own love, and preparing our heart to welcome His forgiveness facilitates the development of humility. It is like terrain that has to be tilled as *humus* in order to be free of thorns and weeds, and manured, so that the heart becomes humble when its sins are tilled away, freed of those thorns and weeds that are our idols; and enriched by the virtues so as to receive God's seed, His Word (the *logos spermatikos*—a word capable of giving life).

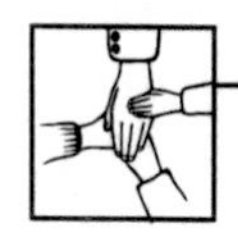

Possible Aids

In this phase, a companion along the way ought to be a manifestation of God's tenderness, open to the suffering of a separated person, and making himself or herself attentive to his or her needs. Like the paralyzed man's four friends (Mark 2:3), acting as *guides to Christ*, a companion ought to:

- Have a heart that knows how to listen to what is expressed and requested in words, but even more to what is not expressed and requested in words.
- "Pray to the Holy Spirit that He give us eyes to see, ears to hear, and hands to work: divine eyes, ears and hands, full of kindness."[23]

Pray for God's holy Mother to help you. She who is Immaculate by grace never forgets she is also a Mother to sinners. Our own state of regeneration and purification is the fruit of her intercession, of her remaining near us. Concretely, strive to:

- Re-create a family environment, especially for those most alone, with no family nearby. Be especially attentive around vacation time: Christmas, Easter, and summer vacation. Know which days the kids spend with the other parent, to help the separated person avoid brooding over feeling excluded from a family reunion they will not share. On such occasions, insist on going out together, invent chance meetings and drop by without warning ("I was just passing by...")
- On the spiritual plane, value the Eucharistic celebration. A deeper catechesis on the Liturgy of the Eucharist is opportune, to live it as a spousal, nuptial encounter. Knowing how to *enjoy* Holy Mass is an important aid for every Christian, but even

[23] Ibidem, p.45.

more for those suffering in general, and for the separated person in particular.* In fact, it is especially during Holy Mass each person can bear his or her own sufferings, presented and offered by the priest to God the Father together with the Eucharistic Sacrifice.

- A spiritual guide can help one to receive loneliness as a time of grace, precisely as a time of engagement with our Lord. It is important to value silence, not merely as an absence of noise, but as a sign of God's presence alongside the one suffering. "Even the nuptial love of Christ and of the Church exists as a time in suspense on account of the great silence of death. Yet this silence is not empty: it guards a mystery which works in the depths, in the abyss of the mystery of God and of His work."[24]

Mistakes to Avoid

Impatience: This is a time in which one passes from a phase of total dejection to one of gradual inner healing and personal reconstruction. Still, one can expect there may be fallout whenever family difficulties arise, or around the holidays.

---

* (English Publisher's note) "The liturgy is the summit toward which the activity of the Church is directed; at the same time it is the font from which all her power flows. For the aim and object of apostolic works is that all who are made sons of God by faith and baptism should come together to praise God in the midst of His Church, to take part in the sacrifice, and to eat the Lord's supper. The liturgy in its turn moves the faithful, filled with 'the paschal sacraments,' to be 'one in holiness'; it prays that 'they may hold fast in their lives to what they have grasped by their faith'; the renewal in the Eucharist of the covenant between the Lord and man draws the faithful into the compelling love of Christ and sets them on fire" (*Sacrosanctum Concilium*, 10).

[24] G. MAZZANTI, Mistero pasquale mistero nuziale, cit., p.43.

Convalescence can be much longer than expected; yet God always brings His work to fulfillment, never leaving unfinished what He has begun to build.

Personal Reflections

- Do I allow myself to be seduced by God?
- Do I truly allow Him to enter my life as Lord?
- Have I ever asked Jesus for a more personal and intimate relationship?
- Do I call on His mother Mary for help?

Here are some readings for meditation:

Hosea 2:16-18

> Therefore, I will allure her now; I will lead her into the wilderness and speak persuasively to her. Then I will give her the vineyards she had, and the valley of Achor as a door of hope. There she will respond as in the days of her youth, as on the day when she came up from the land of Egypt. On that day—oracle of the LORD—You shall call me "My husband," and you shall never again call me "My baal."

Hosea 2:21-25

> I will betroth you to me forever: I will betroth you to me with justice and with judgment, with loyalty and with compassion; I will betroth you to me with fidelity, and you shall know the LORD. On that day I will respond—oracle of the LORD—I will respond to the heavens, and they will respond to the earth; The earth will respond to the grain, and wine, and oil, and these will respond to Jezreel. I will sow her for myself in the land, and I will have pity on Not-Pitied. I will say to Not-My-People, "You are my people," and he will say, "My God!"

THE GROUP

They devoted themselves to the
teaching of the apostles and to the
communal life, to the breaking of the
bread and to the prayers.

Acts 2:42

Goal of the Stage

Self-esteem.

Description of the path

By self-esteem, I do not mean a narcissistic perception of oneself, but rather the healthy and balanced awareness of a person's value.

A person with balanced self-esteem would esteem everyone else and, with this new inner awareness, would relate freely with everyone, without falling into affective co-dependency.

Even if, from the moment of my conception, no one had ever showered me with real feelings of welcome and love, I know for certain that God has called me into existence with love, and for love. The Lord says, "Because you are precious in My eyes and glorious, and because I love you, I give men in return for you and peoples in exchange for your life," (Isaiah 43:4). This is the foundation of self-reconstruction.

One objective to be mindful of is that of helping the separated person become aware of his or her great dignity as a person.

The group can be of help to a separated person living with the acute suffering of abandonment, as well as with a sense of feeling despised and repudiated.

The brotherhood or sisterhood of a group can become a concrete, visible manifestation of that respect and that welcoming love each of us needs, favoring the development of hidden abilities and talents. It is not by chance that St. Paul exhorts in his Letter to the Romans, "love one another with mutual affection; anticipate one another in showing honor" (12:10).

Beyond one's mistakes, everyone is a person worthy of esteem, precious in God's eyes. The story of "Everyman" is a sacred story, to be lived out as a protagonist alongside God, and to fulfill His saving plan of love.

Which group?

A group is useful for different reasons:

- To know real people demonstrating solidarity;
- To grow spiritually by praying together, valuing communal prayer;
- To experience feelings of appreciation for the choices one has made.[25]

That said, it is most appropriate to form groups specifically for separated people who are faithful to the sacrament. In general, for separated persons, the parish community offers some opportunities, which we could arrange into three types:

---

[25] Cf. ITALIAN EPISCOPAL CONFERENCE, *Direttorio di pastorale familiare per la Chiesa in Italia*, cit., nos. 208-209.

- "Generic" prayer groups, or Church movements of a charitable nature, such as Catholic Action, the St. Vincent de Paul Society, volunteering, etc.
- Dual-gender prayer groups, which may include divorced-and-remarried couples;
- Parish ministries such as choir, CCD, Extraordinary Ministers of the Eucharist, etc.

Yet these groups rarely discuss the sacrament of marriage or its mission. So, the separated person may be making a common spiritual journey alongside a baptized person who has never received the sacrament of marriage. In addition, the motivation for which a Christian separated person does not move on to other romantic encounters *more uxorio*[26] can be broken down as follows:

- Not wishing to get caught up in new romantic relationships for fear of further disillusionment. This attitude is reflected by phrases such as, "Enough! What I have gone through is enough."
- Thinking that one is not able to form a new affectively stable relationship. Here phrases like "At this point" get used a lot: "At this point…at my age…At this point the damage is done…" (Yet if the occasion offered itself…)
- Feelings of aversion to the other sex can be awakened, "Men (or women) are all unfaithful, liars…"
- Wishing to remain faithful to the original decision of one's own marriage.

While the person may in fact continue to live alone, more often than not he or she is unaware that the mission continues to exist of advancing in the sacrament of marriage. A consequence of this is to debase and suffocate the sacrament and its mission, with

---

[26] Translator's note: "as if married" (Latin).

indissolubility often coming to be seen and lived by the separated person as a mere norm (practically penal) imposed by the Church.

It is important to reflect, rather, on the fact that one's sacramental marriage is not "over" but *alive*, and that the faithful spouse remains a minister of the grace it provides. So, there exists a privileged stream of grace each of the spouses can approach on the other's behalf, as well as on behalf of the children, or of other relations in general.

It is important to be aware that one remains a minister of the sacrament. If one's spouse is physically and emotionally distant, he or she still remains united to us in spirit, precisely on account of the sacrament's indissolubility. Just as in the Apostles' Creed we claim to believe the communion of the baptized is found within the Holy Spirit, so we likewise affirm that spouses have a spiritual-conjugal union, an exclusive channel of grace proper to the power of the sacrament of marriage.[27]

No other person can access this channel of the couple's grace, not even a priest. Therefore each spouse is always a minister of the other's grace and gift, even when the other fails to respond to it. In the case of separation, the faithful spouse assumes the role of inter-cessor in a special way. One's whole life, lived out in works, in prayer, and in dedication to one's family members, becomes a gift of self to God. Only with this awareness does everything take on meaning: suffering, loneliness, prayer, tears.

The separated person, thus beneficially guided, can render the sacrament more effective in so far as God's plan for one's family comes to be fulfilled, renewed day after day by one's "I do."

From everything examined so far, a targeted pastoral strategy can be deduced for helping separated persons resume anew their role as ministers of the sacrament. For this reason a specific group is most appropriate for this demographic.

---

[27] Cf. *Gaudium et spes* no.48.

In fact, beyond prayer and welcoming, such a group would pursue as a basic objective a formation that values sacramental matrimony, and which investigates more deeply the meaning of indissolubility in the case of separated spouses. In this way, a separated person can arrive freely at a gift of self, acquiring ever more awareness of one's royal, priestly, and prophetic role, preeminently within the family, as an effect of sacramental marriage.

Group components

Besides separated or divorced persons faithful to the sacrament, it is key that the group be formed of married couples involved in pastoral family work, as well as of persons with an adequate preparation in the sacrament of marriage.

A group thus composed is useful for various reasons, beyond that of community prayer:

- One can follow a *path of formation* regarding the sacrament of marriage and the aspect of indissolubility, lending greater consistency to one's choice;
- One grows in the conviction that *forgiveness* is an *indispensable step*, above all for one's own peace, but also for the peace of one's family members;
- A solidarity emerges among members flowing from simple valid advice, even as to educating the children, yet which also can extend to other concrete demands;
- A particular *spiritual union* is born among separated people, sharing the same situation as they do.

Summing up, the objectives of the specific group for separated persons faithful to the sacrament are:

- Welcoming and support;

- Communal prayer;
- Formation in the sacrament of marriage;
- An itinerary of self-esteem founded upon God's Word;
- A journey of forgiveness;
- A renewal of marital commitments.

In the beginning, this last objective can seem onerous, and thus is not obligatory. A separated person may attend meetings just the same, free to decide whether or not to share in that renewal of one's "I do."

Mistakes to Avoid

A very common mistake, be it by a companion on the way, or by other group members, is that of expressing judgments about situations or about persons. The "guilty party" is often sought out, but the real risk here is of being "blind guides, who strain out the gnat and swallow the camel," (Matthew 23:24).

None of us is infallible, and still less are we without sin. Even the absent spouse remains a child of God. "Let the one among you who is without sin cast the first stone…" (John 8:7).

If at the beginning of this journey one allows for the opportunity to vent, it is still absolutely counterproductive to ask further questions which could encourage endless griping.

Personal Reflections

- The group is a small community. Do I share my goods within it?
- Do I value my own dignity, even when I see others who have qualities I lack?
- Do I realize that diversity is a wealth to be respected?
- Do I know what my talents are, so they can bear fruit?

Here are some readings for meditation:

1 Thessalonians 5:11

Therefore, encourage one another and build one another up, as indeed you do.

2 Corinthians 1:3-5

Blessed be the God and Father of our Lord Jesus Christ, the Father of compassion and God of all encouragement, who encourages us in our every affliction, so that we may be able to encourage those who are in any affliction with the encouragement with which we ourselves are encouraged by God. For as Christ is sufferings overflow to us, so through Christ does our encouragement also overflow.

Acts 1:14

All these devoted themselves with one accord to prayer, together with some women, and Mary the mother of Jesus, and His brothers.

Acts 2:46-47

Every day they devoted themselves to meeting together in the temple area and to breaking bread in their homes. They ate their meals with exultation and sincerity of heart, praising God and enjoying favor with all the people. And every day the Lord added to their number those who were being saved.

RECONCILIATION

… as I love you …

John 15:12

Goal of the Stage

To understand forgiveness as a medicine for our wounds. To pray for our spouse

Description of the path

Reconciliation is a behavior which rejuvenates our capacity to love: "The act of forgiveness is always a regenerating and *rejuvenating* act."[28]

It is important to be reconciled with oneself, with others, and with God. We are reconciled with God every time that, recognizing our poverty and our sins, we have recourse to Him to receive the Father's merciful embrace.[*] From this healing, saving,

[28] G. MAZZINI, *Mistero pasquale, mistero nuziale*, cit., p.86.

[*] (English Publisher's note) Regarding the sacrament of reconciliation: "'Those who approach the sacrament of Penance obtain pardon from God's mercy for the offense committed against him, and are, at the same time, reconciled with the Church which they have wounded by their sins and which by charity, by example, and by prayer labors for their conversion'" (Catechism of the Catholic Church 1422, citing *Lumen Gentium* 11 §2). "It is called the *sacrament of*

and gratuitous embrace which restores us to our dignity as God's children, we also receive the capacity to be reconciled with ourselves and with others: with ourselves, because we often lack self-esteem; and with others because we have failed to view them with God's own heart. To be reconciled to the one who has offended us is a basic step in the path of every Christian.

We know that to be separated persons faithful to the sacrament, and not to have forgiven a spouse, is the sign of a merely apparent adhesion to God's will, one which is superficial and sterile.

> When it is observed that the separated person has recovered an awareness of being a child of God, of being a forgiven sinner—being worthy of esteem and *precious in His eyes*—then one can begin to speak of forgiveness.[29]

First, it is important to distinguish *reconciliation* from *cohabitation.* These verbs indicate two distinct actions, and one does not imply the other. To reconcile with one's spouse does not automatically imply cohabitation; especially when conditions both opportune and favorable for reuniting the couple and the family have yet to exist (not to mention the possibility of grave moral impediments).

Still, reconciliation is important just the same for one's own peace and spiritual growth. What are the qualities of forgiveness Jesus describes (cf. Matthew 18:35)? One characteristic of forgiveness is that it be unconditional. The person who wounds us is restored to his or her place even when we know that, humanly speaking, he or she can still err, and so wound us again. "This is a

---

Reconciliation, because it imparts to the sinner the love of God who reconciles: 'Be reconciled to God.' He who lives by God's merciful love is ready to respond to the Lord's call: 'Go; first be reconciled to your brother.'" (CCC 1424, citing *2 Cor.* 5:20 and *Mt.* 5:24)

[29] *Un cammino cristiano per i separati*, p.51.

tough commitment, and at first just the idea of having to do it can upset us."[30]

It is not easy to perform this gesture, above all due to the defenses and psychological resistance we have constructed around our ego throughout the course of our lives. Yet, as always, what is impossible for us is possible for God. So it is only through prayer and asking God for the gift to be able to do this that we can be merciful, as our heavenly Father is merciful.

Besides, we should recognize we, too, have been forgiven by God *seventy times seven times*. Every time, that is, that we have wounded Him with our sin. Another characteristic of forgiveness, then, is that of being unlimited.

Still, even if we understand we have to forgive from the heart, we likewise need to be aware that we cannot. How many times do we say:

> "I would like to forgive, but I cannot." Even in this case it is important to distinguish between the terms *want* and *able to*. Even in this case what is asked of us is the *want*; the *ability* is from God. Forgiveness from the heart is a gift, one we can receive only from God, precisely for the purpose of sharing it. So:
>
> - ❖ The first step is to *decide* to forgive
> - ❖ The second step is to ask God for the gift of being able to forgive
> - ❖ The third step is to begin to pray for the one who has hurt us
>
> One will then be able to observe the fruits within oneself, feeling at peace within, as well as becoming able to ask forgiveness of others for own lack of tact and charity.[31]

---

[30] Ibidem.

[31] Ibidem.

Forgiveness given, and sought, is the healing balm for a wounded relationship.

A behavior with strong healing capacity is forgiveness. Though a lot is written and preached about forgiveness just about every day, it is much less practiced. It is inevitable that among people living under the same roof there may be tension, misunderstanding, or squabbling. When we have been offended, we know we are supposed to forgive; but it is not enough for us to be convinced of this to offer our forgiveness.

It is not enough to say, "You offended me, but I forgive you." This phrase does not produce a healing effect.

Such an expression does not satisfy anyone. We would feel guilty and wounded, so it is not healing. In fact, a defense mechanism could graft itself onto us whereby we seek to relieve ourselves of responsibility to others, quickly rejecting a forgiveness, which so patronizingly descends from on high. Another non-healing response could be provoked by forgiveness offered under certain conditions. We say we are disposed to forgive "'if…if…if…"

But, this is just a truce under talks.

So how do you do it, then? Already the word 'for-*give*' helps us understand what is given is a *gift for*…its nature is to be gratuitous.

For this fact of forgiveness, Jesus is both master and model, such as when, newly risen, He finds Peter on the Lake of Tiberius (John 21:15-17). Jesus does not say, 'You betrayed Me three times, but I forgive you just the same.' In this beautiful passage from John's Gospel, Jesus asks Peter if he loves Him and, receiving an affirmative response each time, He reconfirms him in the role already entrusted to him:

> You are Peter, and upon this rock I will build my Church, and the gates of the netherworld shall not prevail against it. I will give you the keys to the kingdom of heaven. Whatever you

bind on earth shall be bound in heaven; and whatever you loose on earth shall be loosed in heaven, (Matthew 16:18-19).

The third time Peter feels skewered, but it is a restorative skewering, as it lights a fire under him to get back up and serve the Master. This healing aspect which emerges is a *reaffirmation of trust* in the one who has wounded us, all the while remaining aware that, as a human being, he or she may stumble again. The Gospel of Matthew (18:21-22) is relevant here and it is interesting to note that it is actually Peter who asks the question: "'Lord, if my brother sins against me, how often must I forgive him? As many as seven times?" Jesus answered, 'I say to you, not seven times but seventy-seven times.'"

So, offering forgiveness is not circumscribed to a finite number of occasions, but rather is *unlimited.*

Another healing aspect of forgiveness lies in its being *extenuating*. This should not be confused with a do-goodism viewing everything as okay. In fact, the forgiveness recognizes the error, the offense, the sin, while relieving the other's burden by forbearing with the one responsible. Jesus teaches us this when He prays for His persecutors from the cross, "Father, forgive them, they know not what they do" (Luke 23:34).

"The cross was Christ's throne in this world."[32]

It is here one reaches the summit of Jesus' teachings on forgiveness.

"When you stand to pray, forgive anyone against whom you have a grievance, so that your heavenly Father may in turn forgive you your transgressions," (Mark 11:25); "love your enemies, and pray for those who persecute you," (Matthew 5:44).

Jesus not only prays for us. He justifies us.

---

[32] Discourse of His Holiness John Paul II to the Cardinals of the Ordinary Consistory, 2001.

Summing up, we could say forgiveness has the following characteristics: it is *unconditional*, reaffirming the person forgiven in his or her role; *unlimited*; and *extenuating*.

> It is only from an attitude aware of being the sign of God's love in the world that such forgiveness can spring, since God's own love for the sinner is unconditional, unlimited, and justifying. No one can forgive from the heart without these two inner motives: deciding to forgive, and asking God for the power to do so. Then one will see the fruit; i.e., when the one offended against, the one offending, and the relation between the two are all restored.[33]

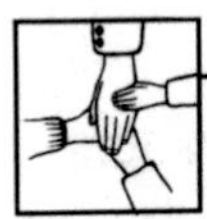

Possible Aids

Here are some suggestions. A community can help a brother or sister to:

- "Cultivate the need to forgive which is inherent in Christian love, and perhaps to be ready to return to one's former married life";[34]
- Pray for one's spouse;
- Have Masses offered for one's spouse;
- Organize a forgiveness-themed Liturgy with suitable Scripture passages, and pray for forgiveness before the Blessed Sacrament.[35]

---

[33] G. CAMPANELLA, *Familigia, comunitá sanante*, tesi di diploma in Pastorale della salute, Gymnasium Charitatis Religiosi Camilliani, Caltanissetta, 1999-2001.

[34] *Familiaris Consortio* no.83.

[35] *Un cammino cristiano per i separati*, cit., p.77.

Here are some readings for meditation:

Matthew 5:44-48

> But I say to you, love your enemies, and pray for those who persecute you, that you may be children of your heavenly Father, for He makes His sun rise on the bad and the good, and causes rain to fall on the just and the unjust. For if you love those who love you, what recompense will you have? Do not the tax collectors do the same? And if you greet your brothers only, what is unusual about that? Do not the pagans do the same? So be perfect, just as your heavenly Father is perfect.

Luke 6:27-29

> But to you who hear I say, love your enemies, do good to those who hate you, bless those who curse you, pray for those who mistreat you. To the person who strikes you on one cheek, offer the other one as well, and from the person who takes your cloak, do not withhold even your tunic.

RENEWAL OF THE "I DO"

"Set me as a seal upon your heart,"

Song of Songs 8:6

Goal of the Stage

To become aware of the task of marriage ministry.

Description of the path

After having accepted the cross, and being surrendered to His love, we wish to renew our nuptial "I do" to the Lord.

"It seems absurd to renew the marital 'I do' without one's spouse present, yet the promises we made the day of our marriage we made before God, and our 'I do' has its home in His Heart."[36]

The renewal of an "I do" is not an act of sheer human will power, but flows from the saving "I do" of Jesus. Only by remaining in Christ can we renew our "I do," resulting in a reflection of that unique "I do" pronounced by the Trinity.

If in virtue of our baptism we Christians profess the communion of saints, must we not likewise affirm spouses are

[36] Ibidem, p.61.

granted, through the sacrament of marriage, an exclusive spiritual-spousal union?[37]

To offer an image—mundane, alas, but perhaps useful—we might imagine the sacrament of marriage as a joint bank account which, the day we got married, God opened for us in the bank of His love. Only my spouse and I can access this account, and it was opened by God's love.

When a spouse fails to exercise his or her right to it, the other, faithful, spouse can still make *withdrawals* from this account, which is truly special: the more you take, the more there is. To access this private account requires renewing that "I do" we pronounced the day of our wedding, kept safe within God's Heart.

Precisely in virtue of this grace, which proceeds from God, we have the task of praying and interceding for our spouse and for our children.

With a heightened and broader awareness we again can assume our role as minister of the marriage sacrament, because we are now more aware that there exists an *exclusive stream of grace which I alone, as a spouse, can access*. No other person, not even a priest, can access this stream.

> Even if one's spouse and children walk on other paths far from God, to us is entrusted the task, and the privilege, of interceding like Moses on the mountain top.[38]

> …do not destroy your people, the heritage you redeemed in your greatness and have brought out of Egypt…
> (Deuteronomy 9:26).
>
> If I find favor with you, Lord, please, Lord, come along in our company. This is indeed a stiff-necked people; yet pardon our wickedness and sins, and claim us as your own, (Exodus 34:9).

---

[37] Cf. *Gaudium et spes*, no.48.

[38] COMUNITÀ DI CARESTO, *Un cammino cristiano per i separati*, cit., p. 62.

If in virtue of baptism we believe in the *communion sanctorum* (communion of saints), how much more must there exist a spiritual-conjugal union in virtue of marital indissolubility? Such is the *communio coniugum* (communion of spouses).

> Indissolubility is like a stream connecting God's heart to the two spouses, and that spouse who remains faithful does nothing other than pour out sanctifying grace upon the other.[39]

We do not know in what mysterious ways this may be fulfilled, yet everything:

> given by God is never lost; time, sacrifices, prayers, tears. All this, poured out in the grace of the sacrament, is like a subterranean stream, you do not see it, yet it flows silently, giving life and fruitfulness to plants and trees alike.[40]

The marriage has not failed, because a sacrament cannot fail. The sacrament is alive, and the faithful spouse continues to render it effective with his or her daily "I do." Even today, it is *"I thee wed."* My husband is my husband always, never my ex-husband; my wife is always my wife, never my ex-wife!

One's spouse is entrusted to us by God Himself, who asks us to love and forgive the other. We remain custodians of this. We can refuse, and the Lord may save him or her just the same, yet we lose the chance to cooperate in God's saving plan. "To renew the 'I do' therefore is to broaden our stream and receive a greater grace for one's spouse, for the children"– and for us.[41]

> To renew the "I do," is a witness to the world that is *a rugged and difficult path to follow* because it goes against the current yet,

---

[39] Ibidem, p.61.

[40] Ibidem, p.59.

[41] Ibidem, p.62.

when one is supported by a community, the path can be happier.[42]

Our choice is not a *generic* witness, but a presence, *the presence of the invincible community of God*.[43] The witness of a life becomes the visible sign of God's work in His mortal, sinful creature, through the grace this sacrament offers spouses.

> To be Christians is to imitate the total "yes" of Jesus to the Father, and to receive from Him the grace to go to the extreme of His "yes" in loving one's brethren. Our "I do" is something first spoken at our baptism; we enter thus into a covenant with God, and of loving our brothers unto the end, including our enemies.
>
> As on the day of one's marriage the baptized solemnly say "I do," and their "I do" becomes the sacrament of an eternally faithful "yes" of Jesus to the Church, His spouse.
>
> In the inevitable difficulties of conjugal life Jesus, who is committed to us, helps spouses confront their trials and say "I do" every day. When a separation or divorce occurs, it is still He who helps the faithful spouse take this wild journey (which, humanly, he or she would not be capable of) and renew the "I do" to one's own spouse.
>
> To know the happiness of the Beatitudes in their fullness, there is no other path than that of the cross, which flows on to the resurrection, passing through an "I do" without reserve to the love of the Father, and to love of one's brethren. This is why, in all its paradox, the path of renewing an "I do" to one's spouse is the path of freedom, of healing, and of true happiness.[44]

---

[42] Ibidem, p.59.

[43] Cf. G. MAZZANTI, *Mistero pasquale mistero pasquale*, cit., p.87.

[44] Cf. COMMUNION NOTRE-DAME DE L'ALLIANCE, *Le renouvellement du oui au conjoint*, Introduction.

Commitments of the separated spouse

The mission of the sacrament of marriage requires not only avoiding other romantic relationships, but even:

- Being a custodian for the other. One's spouse has been entrusted to us by God, and every time we say "I do," we renew the grace of the sacrament given exclusively to us.
- Praying for one's spouse daily, invoking the Spirit's spousal love;
- Participating in the Eucharistic celebration as a minister of the sacrament, interceding, asking God the Father to pour out on one's spouse the grace which flows from the sacrifice of Jesus Christ, as well as asking the same for the children;
- Having Holy Masses offered for one's spouse;
- Speaking well of one's spouse, or else remaining silent. It can be a grave sin to speak ill of one's spouse, or to recount negative things about him or her, even when true;
- Educating one's children in forgiveness;
- Reactivating more peaceful behaviors within the relationship;
- Having Holy Masses said for any person to whom one's spouse has become attached; since even he or she is a child of God.

In day-to-day life, and whenever there is time, the separated person should practice charity in those situations one is called to do so: first as a family member, but also in general as a Christian. For example:

- Strengthening family relationships;
- Assisting one's elderly or sick family members. At times, it may happen, we neglect family members to dedicate time to strangers;

- Supporting other separated persons who are still experiencing the darkest phases of the separation experience;
- Being a "living stone" in one's parish (1 Peter 2:5), patiently overcoming any distrust or prejudice one may continue to encounter. Most sensible parishes promote attending formation meetings on the Church's Magisterium. It may also be possible to serve as an extraordinary minister of Holy Communion, catechist, lector, or choir member;
- Becoming a volunteer, after proper training, in various areas of the Church's life: families, the sick, the disabled, the poor, etc.

At this point, our home, which at the beginning was a wreck, has now been renovated by God's own hand. To me the most appropriate image is that of a castle on a high mountain, with a much broader horizon looking out upon creation. It is no longer night. There is a soft, delicate early morning light; the air is limpid. The castle is a tent-shaped gazebo covered by veils with the colors of dawn, open on all four sides. Under the canopy, in the middle, is a small column bearing a monstrance with the Eucharistic Jesus exposed, who is God-with-us. *"And behold, I am with you always, until the end of the age"* (Matthew 28:20).

Personal Reflections

- It feels as though only I am a minister of grace of the marriage sacrament on behalf of the whole family. Do I want to ask the Lord to help me renew my "I do" every day?
- Do I share with the group that dimension of exclusivity this ministry shares, which is entrusted to us in marriage?

Here are some readings for meditation:

John Paul II's *Letter to Families*, nos.18-19

Matthew 9:15

Jesus answered them, "Can the wedding guests mourn as long as the bridegroom is with them? The days will come when the bridegroom is taken away from them, and then they will fast."

John 2:1-10

On the third day there was a wedding in Cana in Galilee, and the mother of Jesus was there. Jesus and His disciples were also invited to the wedding. When the wine ran short, the mother of Jesus said to Him, "They have no wine." Jesus said to her, "Woman, how does your concern affect Me? My hour has not yet come." His mother said to the servers, "Do whatever He tells you." Now there were six stone water jars there for Jewish ceremonial washings, each holding twenty to thirty gallons.

Jesus told them, "Fill the jars with water." So they filled them to the brim. Then He told them, "Draw some out now and take it to the headwaiter." So they took it. And when the headwaiter tasted the water that had become wine, without knowing where it came from (although the servers who had drawn the water knew), the headwaiter called the bridegroom and said to him, "Everyone serves good wine first, and then when people have drunk freely, an inferior one; but you have kept the good wine until now."

Revelation 21: 9-14

One of the seven angels who held the seven bowls filled with the seven last plagues came and said to me, "Come here. I will show you the bride, the wife of the Lamb." He took me in spirit to a great, high mountain and showed me the holy city Jerusalem coming down out of heaven from God. It gleamed with the splendor of God. Its radiance was like that of a precious stone, like jasper, clear as crystal. It had a massive, high wall, with twelve gates where twelve angels were stationed and on which names were inscribed, (the names) of the twelve tribes of the Israelites. There were three gates facing east, three north, three south, and three west. The wall of the city had twelve courses of stones as its foundation, on which were inscribed the twelve names of the twelve apostles of the Lamb.

Only I

Who, if not I,
Is the minister of the sacrament?

Who, if not I,
Prays for you, the absent one?

Who, if not I,
Offers up suffering for you?

I alone, in God,
Can give you what no one else
Can ever give you.

THE GIFT OF SELF

I come with an inscribed scroll
written upon me.
I delight to do your will,

Psalm 40:8-9

Goal of the Stage

To become a sign of God's merciful love.

Description of the path

God, who is eternal life itself, has chosen the path of incarnation to redeem man, a mortal and sinful creature, to save him from death and render him immortal and holy in accord with an ancient plan.

> One may consider the fact that Christ wishes to live the reality of *una caro* (one flesh) with the corrupted/sinful flesh of humanity. He can descend and meet humanity as a body of flesh, as one of humanity.[45]

Only through a mortal body could Christ descend, defeat death and raise the dead, giving us immortality. Suffering in His

[45] G. MAZZANTI, *Mistero pasquale mistero nuziale*, cit., p.52.

flesh the consequences of our sin of disobedience, He redeems us from our condition as sinners.

Making us one body in Him by means of the marriage of the Lamb, He gives us the gift of His divine nature, which makes us holy.

Through the incarnation, Jesus renders visible and concrete His offering to the Father, and in His offering on the cross, He reveals the Father's merciful love to us.

Christ on the cross is both a gift of Self to the Father for our redemption, and a gift of the merciful Father to the sinner, to redeem us.

> The exodus/gift of the Son from the Trinity could have been "peaceful"; in fact it was not, because the gift encountered a rejection which nevertheless has remained God's gift. The surrender of Christ (be it that of the Father or His own!) does not occur in an idyllic manner but, rather, dramatically.[46]

A gift of self is offered to God the Father for sinners. Jesus, as He surrenders Himself voluntarily to His persecutors, offers Himself to the Father for them.

> At the last supper, Christ, the Spouse, gives Himself to a community that betrays Him. But also, *because* it betrays Him, Christ places Himself into the hand of those who will abandon Him; He gives Himself to one who will deny Him, and to one who will "begin" His death.
>
> ...But in a certain sense, it is precisely the dramatic reality of human rejection which renders His gift more authentic; it both renders it, and reveals it to be, entirely pure, totally and absolutely gratuitous.[47]

---

[46] Ibidem, p.35.

[47] Ibidem., p.26.

We too, are placed in the hands of a spouse who now denies us, and who thus initiates our death. For some of us, our spouse not only no longer wishes to be our spouse, but wishes to kill within us the fact of our being his or her spouse, thereby denying us.

We are a *dead spouse.*

> Yet death is not definitive destruction. It is a wounding of relationships. Beneath the ashes ("You are ashes/dust, and to dust/ashes you will return") yet burns the secret of divine life…the river of underground life is not exhausted. It flows on in silence.[48]

We are wounded spouses, suffering but alive, because our sacrament is alive. Therefore, our priestly, royal, and prophetic work continues within the family. It is only united to Christ in the Spirit that we, too, can offer ourselves to God the Father:

- Jesus, for the salvation of all;
- Ourselves, as ministers of the sacrament, interceding for the conversion of our spouse and our children.

> For to this you have been called, because Christ also suffered for you, leaving you an example that you should follow in His footsteps (1 Peter 2:21).
>
> Now I rejoice in my sufferings for your sake, and in my flesh I am filling up what is lacking in the afflictions of Christ on behalf of His Body, which is the Church (Colossians 1:24).

"The wound inflicted becomes the opening to a gift."[49] The wound becomes a home, welling up into love.

---

[48] Ibidem, p.50.

[49] Ibidem, p.34.

This implies knowing how to transform the wound into an act of love. Precisely what wounds us is that through which we can love yet more. The act which has wounded/killed you becomes an act of love: it is the paradoxical rebirth of the happy fault.[50]

Things which have occurred can bear a surplus of life and love. There is no calculation, only the truth about love.[51]

The gift of self is gratuitous: there is no calculation, but only the truth about love. This is the paradox of the divine gift: from the mortal wound arises life for the one who injures.

This is what remains inconceivable for "doubting Thomases."

The wounds inflicted on Christ by humanity are exactly the same wounds through which Christ loves the humanity which has denied Him. The Risen One transmutes these wounds from an element of death into an element of life, from an element of betrayal into the sign of a faithful love which bypasses and overcomes humanity's rejection and fragile love.[52]

It is precisely these wounds which yield life and glory. Christ surpasses and transforms these wounds. They go from being a humiliating sign of homicidal rejection and denial, to the sign and guarantee of a greater love precisely for those people who have inflicted the wounds. "My love for you is no joke." This is a "love stronger than death."[53]

The gift of self stems from a love which is not of human nature, but of divine nature, and therefore may be received only from God. In fact, in welcoming Divine Love, we are capable of hoping beyond all hope, of loving without being

[50] Translator's note: the reference is to the Easter Proclamation (*Exsultet*), which speaks of Adam and Eve's fall as in some way a "happy fault" (*felix culpa*), because it won for us "so great a redeemer."

[51] Ibidem, p.86.

[52] Ibidem, p.75.

[53] Translator's note: the reference is to Song of Songs 8:6.

> repaid, of knowing how to remain, to commiserate, to forebear and to forgive those who will not be forgiven.[54]

Only the love of God can be *eros-agape*, that is, a love of yearning *and* of offering.

> We have seen that God's *eros* for man is also totally *agape*. This is not only because it is bestowed in a completely gratuitous manner, without any previous merit, but also because it is a love which forgives. Hosea, above all, shows us this *agape* dimension of God's love for us goes far beyond the aspect of gratuity. Israel has committed "adultery" and broken the Covenant; God should judge and repudiate her. It is precisely at this point God is revealed to be God and not human. "How can I give you up, O Ephraim! How can I hand you over, O Israel!...My heart recoils within Me, My compassion grows warm and tender. I will not execute my fierce anger, I will not again destroy Ephraim; for I am God and not man, the Holy One in your midst" (Hosea 11:8-9). God's passionate love for his people—for humanity—is at the same time a forgiving love. It is so great that it turns God against Himself, His love against His justice. Here Christians can see a dim prefigurement of the mystery of the Cross. So great is God's love for man that, by becoming man He follows him even into death, thus reconciling justice and love…[55]

Divine love is defenseless and moves on to a gift of self; it is inexhaustible even when the other fails to reciprocate; it is merciful and thus, already, has forgiven even before the other has repented.

Divine love rejected and unwelcome becomes crucified love, a silent offering presented to the Father, a total oblation.

---

[54] *Un cammino cristiano per i separati*, p.78.

[55] BENEDICT XVI, Encyclical Letter *Deus Caritas Est* ("God is Love"), Libreria Editrice Vaticana, sec. 10.

The gift is Christ Himself living and in agony (*agon* = fight) on the cross. The *sarx* (flesh) in which He is incarnated is itself a prayer raised to God, a sacrifice immaculate and offered to God for our redemption, a wonder to adore.

It is wonder at an omnipotent God who becomes imposing, of an innocent God who bears our sins, of a God eternally loving of the sinner to whom He continues to present the gift of His total love, gratuitous and defenseless.

"On that same tree is hung death and, arising unexpectedly from it, life."[56]

The gift of self is total, without reserve, irreversible, of all our physical, psychological, and spiritual faculties *hic et nunc* (here and now). To leave all our human plans for marriage in God's hands is to become servants of God's own loving plan. The gift of self is without end…"He loved them to the end" (John 13:1).

> To relive the experience of the crucified one, risen again, brings to fruition in spouses the ability to know how to wait out death, beyond any tunnel of death and escape. To be prepared for afterwards, for the moment of being "awoken." "Woman, has no one condemned you?"[57]
>
> The father who awaits us at home is quick to produce party attire as if nothing had happened…for you! (Luke 15).
>
> It is like being present at someone's waking up after surgery, when the other finds you present and close. He or she might do this with a glance or a handclasp, but the point is: You are there. It is like finding that person after waking up from a coma. It is like relocating a person you love after a natural catastrophe.[58]

---

[56] G. MAZZANTI, *Mistero pasquale mistero nuziale*, cit., p.43.

[57] The reference is to John 8:10.

[58] Ibidem, p.85.

> The paschal tragedy educates one in *knowing how to keep* hoping against all hope; learning how not to give in. In your every escape, in every "night," He is always near you. He is that tenacious lifeline which prevents one's overwhelming and definitive self-destruction: "Though you pass through the netherworld, I will not let you go through *hell*."[59]

The gift of self is not an end in itself, but is eschatological: this time granted us by the Lord serves to prepare us for the eternal wedding night of the Lamb, so we can weave for our spouse, and our children, those white vestments of pure, shining linen which alone are proper attire for the (eternal) wedding feast (Revelation 19:8).

Personal Reflections

The gift of self is that summit toward which all those baptized into Christ are called. Each one, in accord with his or her vocation, makes a gift of him or herself to the Father so His loving plan for everyone is aided by our works in day-to-day life.

The separated spouse faithful to the sacrament makes a gift of him or herself to God through his or her spouse and children in a special way. However, this is not all.

The gift of self is offered to strengthen Christian couples in fidelity to their proper sacrament. This offering is made by priests as well, so they can remain faithful to their own sacrament of Holy Orders.

[59] Ibidem.

> The fruit of all the sacraments belongs to all the faithful. All the sacraments are sacred links uniting the faithful with one another and binding them to Jesus Christ.[60]

> Regarding the communion of saints:

> The term "communion of saints" refers also to the communion of "holy persons" (*sancti*) in Christ who "died for all," so what each one does or suffers in, and for, Christ bears fruit for all.[61]

Here are some readings for meditation:

Matthew 5:16

> Just so, your light must shine before others, that they may see your good deeds and glorify your heavenly Father.

John 3:21

> But whoever lives the truth comes to the light, so that his works may be clearly seen as done in God.

---

[60] Catechism of the Catholic Church 950.

[61] Catechism of the Catholic Church 961.

CONCLUSION

The separated or divorced spouse who remains alone, as well as his or her family, are not second class Christians.

They are not like perfectly spherical pearls with which you can make a beautiful necklace; they are oval pearls which, on account of their non-spherical form, are used by jewel smiths to create a unique, and thus even more valuable, jewel.

God the Creator is the only artist who can transform our poor human stories into something unique. In this nuptial/Paschal/Pentecostal event, the loving, delicate, caring, and active presence of Mary comes to our aid.

With characteristically maternal attention, it is she who realizes what is missing and who, as at Cana, tells Jesus the wine is gone (cf. John 2:1-10). It is time to serve the *good* wine. Mary exhorts us to not remain passive, but to be active: "Do whatever He tells you."

Jesus tells us to fill the stone jars with water. These are our hearts of stone which must be purified, so that water can become wine. This wine can become the Eucharistic Blood.

Behold Lord,
I wish to refill these jars
With the tears
Of rejected spouses
And of innocent children betrayed.
They are so many, yet, I am sure,
You have gathered them all up.
But if this is not enough
I ask your Mother
To add her own.
And you, divine Spouse,
Because the Wedding feast isn't over,
To offer Your Own Blood
For the new and eternal Covenant,
So as to transform our pain
Into joy.

"We are unprofitable servants; we have done what we were obliged to do" (Luke 17:10); and that for which we were created: to love.

RENEWAL OF THE "I DO"*

Prayer for the Marriage Vows Renewal

Holy Father, I give you thanks
Because in Your plan of salvation
You have called me to the vocation of marriage,
You have joined my life to that of my companion
So that our union could become a visible sign
Of the union between Christ and His Church.
We were separated,
Perhaps, at least partially, because of my own weakness.
Yet I believe that Christ's love for His Church
Remains faithful and lasting,
Notwithstanding the sins of mankind.
I believe that You have the power to renew
that which has become old.
I ask You, therefore, to forgive my sins,
To mend that which we have attempted to break,
To reconstruct that what sin has destroyed,
And to renew, through the Holy Spirit's grace
My love for he/she whom you have given me
As my inseparable companion
And as a symbol of your presence.
Amen

---

* These prayers were written by Father Pietro Sorci, professor of liturgy at the Pontifical Theological Faculty of Sicily. Before renewing their matrimonial yes, those separated should reflect on the mission of the sacrament of marriage.

Marriage Vows Renewal is also published by the Pontifical Council of the Family. Home >People >Separated Divorce and New Unions. 30 September 2014. www.familiam.org/famiglia_eng/people/00009038_Renewal_of_the_Yes.html

Intercessions*

✝ Let us invoke God the Father, source of true love
So that in the name of Christ He will answer our prayer.

R. *God of love and peace, hear our prayer.*

You who are full and perfect unity of life
And communion of love with Your Son and with the Holy Spirit,
Renew in these spouses the grace of the sacrament
And rekindle in them the flame of your love.
Let us pray. **R.**

You have set out the course of human events
In order to allow us to participate in the cross
And in the glory of Christ:
Allow these spouses to adhere to Your will with all their hearts
By accepting with faith the joys and pains of life..
Let us pray. **R.**

You have created man and woman
In Your image and likeness
So that, by loving each other with all their hearts
They may become the image of the unity of the Holy Trinity,
Allow engaged couples to prepare themselves seriously
To form families according to the spirit of the Gospel.
Let us pray. **R.**

You have established a new state of Christian life
Through the covenant of marriage:
Allow Christian spouses to be witnesses
Of the love of Your Son throughout the world.
Let us pray. **R.**

---

* (English Publisher's note) Intercessions would be suitable for Eucharistic Adoration. See page 105. Original Italian showed title as *Preghiera universale.*

Prayer for Separated Faithful

(Prayer for those spouses present who wish to remain faithful to the marriage covenant)

Holy Father,
You live with the Son and with the Holy Spirit
In a perfect unity of Love.
You have created man and woman
In Your own image and likeness,
And through the Passover of Your Son,
You have made their unity
A visible sign of the covenant that unites Christ to the Church.
We pray to You for these spouses
Who You have sanctified through the sacrament of marriage.
They have experienced the bitterness
And the disappointment of separation,
But they believe with all their hearts
In Your love without regret,
And they wish to remain faithful to the marriage covenant
Which You have consecrated.
Heal their wounds through the grace of the Holy Spirit,
Who renews the face of the earth,
Render them capable of forgiveness,
Do not allow their hearts to become dull,
But, instead, through their words, their works and their lives,
Allow them to become witnesses
In the Church and in the world
Of Your Love,
Which is stronger than sin and death.
We ask You this through our Lord, Jesus Christ, who is God,
And who lives and reigns with You
Together with the Holy Spirit
For ever and ever.
Amen.

APPENDIX

DISCERNING IN SPECIFIC SITUATIONS

The *Directory of Family Ministry for the Church in Italy*[62] and documents of the Church's Magisterium speak of difficult or irregular situations. It is important to make a clear distinction, not for purposes of discrimination, but to be able to propose a path for those who are eligible.

'Difficult' situations include:

- Couples married with the sacrament, not separated, but experiencing relationship difficulties;
- Separated and divorced people who were not morally responsible for the separation, and who do not engage in a new relationship *more uxorio* ["as if married"];

'Irregular' situations include:

- Remarried divorced persons;
- Spouses married civilly;
- Couples living together.

---

[62] ITALIAN EPISCOPAL CONFERENCE, *Direttorio di pastorale familiare per la Chiesa in Italia*, cit.

Besides these, there exist situations of separated and divorced persons who *are* morally responsible for the separation, even if they are not remarried or cohabiting with another.

In each case, the Church has the task of welcoming in charity every one of the baptized, in whatever condition he or she finds himself or herself. Yet it is also an act of love on the part of pastoral workers to be close by, so as to help a person clarify his or her own responsibilities. A priest may discern the situation in which the separated person is living, and propose a specific path for his or her spiritual growth.

The path proposed in this book is adapted only to the case of separated or divorced persons not technically ("morally") responsible for the separation or the divorce.

For a person who has suffered from separation or divorce, or who had to have recourse to it for grave reasons, the *Directory of Family Ministry for the Church in Italy* in numbers 208 and 209 indicates how the community must help in this difficult situation:

> ...the Christian community, beginning with the priests and particularly perceptive married couples, *should make themselves present*, attentively, discretely, and in solidarity.
>
> - Above all, they should value the witness to fidelity of an innocent spouse who bears with all this, accommodating the suffering and solitude which the new situation introduces;
> - They should support the separated spouse, especially when innocent, in his or her pain and solitude, inviting him or her with charity and prudence to share in community life; this would make it easier to overcome the not infrequent temptation to retreat from everything and everybody so as to close in on oneself;
> - Offer respect, understanding, open-hearted solidarity and concrete help, especially at those times when the temptation might grow stronger to pass from solitude to divorce, and then on to a civil marriage;

- Help them to "cultivate the need for forgiveness proper to Christian love, and the readiness to perhaps return to married life as it was before."

> This situation does not preclude one from admission to the sacraments. In its own way, in fact, the condition of separated persons is still a proclamation of the value of the indissolubility of marriage. Obviously, their own participation in the sacraments commits one to being sincerely prompt to forgive, as well as willing to ask questions about whether or not to resume married life.

For divorced persons neither remarried nor living together, in numbers 210 and 211 the *Directory of Family Ministry for the Church in Italy* offers the following indications:

> The Church's pastoral care requires taking into consideration the situation of *divorced persons not remarried* as well. However, insofar as possible, it is important to distinguish between the case of a spouse who has suffered divorce, and who has accepted it constrained by serious reasons to do so bound up with one's own good or that of the children; and that of the spouse who has requested and obtained a divorce as a consequence of their own morally incorrect behavior.
>
> In any case, each spouse must be reminded it is only for the most serious of reasons one should resign oneself to accept divorce, or have recourse to it. In each case divorce amounts only to a separation, one which does not break the conjugal bond.
>
> Regarding the *one who has suffered divorce*, who has accepted it, or who has had recourse to it constrained by serious reasons, but who does not allow him or herself to become involved in a new union, and who commits him or herself to the fulfillment of his or her own family duties and Christian responsibilities, the Christian community:

- Expresses all *esteem*, in the awareness that his or her example of fidelity and Christian consistency is worthy of respect, and assumes a particular value of testimony for other families;
- Lives a method of concrete *solidarity* through closeness and support, even of an economic kind if necessary, especially where young children or minors are involved.

Regarding *admission to the sacraments*, there are no obstacles, "if civil divorce remains the only way possible to ensure certain legitimate rights, be it the care of the children or the protection of the family's savings, it may be tolerated, without constituting a moral fault." "(B)eing forced to suffer a divorce means having received a violence and a humiliation, which renders it all the more necessary, on the Church's part, to provide the witness of her love and help."

In sum, the separated person technically (*moralmente*) responsible for the separation or the divorce, even if he or she lives alone, must be helped to resume Christian life again. It is a question of acting as an aid, "be it for the eventual resumption of married life together, be it for overcoming the possible temptation of passing on to another marriage. In either case, it is a question of always being a support for someone's Christian life."[63]

For all the other cases:

- Divorced and remarried;
- Married only civilly;
- Cohabiting,

the *Directory of Family Ministry for the Church in Italy* offers precise indications on possible paths of accompaniment (cf. nn.212ff).

Therefore, anyone wishing to know of other possible pastoral interventions should see the text cited.

---

[63] Ibidem, no.212.

TESTIMONIES

Spousal testimonies

A love greater than separation

My name is Rosy and I am 39. I have been separated for five and a half years, since my husband decided to leave me with two children (now 3 and 9), to go live with another woman. I tried in every way to avoid separation and tearing up the family, imploring my spouse not to leave, trying to make him reflect on the indissolubility of the sacrament. Unfortunately, nothing worked to stop him and, I find myself alone and deeply humiliated.

Living without my spouse's presence is like suffering the amputation of a part of my body. I have passed through moments of deep pain and distress, and at times truly have thought of not being able to go on. I have sought to find within myself a kind of equilibrium, above all through my faith.

I have refilled my loneliness with interior prayer, asking Christ every day to take more root in me all the time, and to give me the strength needed to keep going.

I must bear witness that the Lord never abandons us and so, one day, during a time of special distress, I found a separated woman like myself. Listening to her words, I felt we were in sync, that we were united by the same spirit, by Christ's love, which transcends all separation and rejection by anyone. I understood that a greater Love existed than separation and betrayal, the true and pure love of God, and that it is offered in a total manner precisely in separation ("I love you even when you don't love me.")

From that moment my life has been on the upswing.

I started attending *Renewal in the Spirit* prayer groups, with which I meet weekly. Besides this, together with other separated persons, we have started a group of prayer and formation to support our fidelity to the sacrament.

With this testimony, I wish to say to my separated brothers and sisters that the separations we suffer must be seen as the Lord's plan for each of us. This cross the Lord has given us, in the measure we are able to bear it, is the cross which makes us sharers in His plan of salvation for us and for our spouses, who are spiritually ill.

Rosy

The trial that strengthens one's faith

From the beginning, when my path of faith got started (around ten years ago), I have always been conscious of the fact that the more one draws closer to the Lord, the more one is subjected to the devil's traps. "My son, when you come to serve the Lord, prepare yourself for trials" (Sirach 2:1). This is especially so if this path is followed by a husband and wife together, since the family is the earthly image of the Most Holy Trinity within God's plan.

After twenty years of marriage—of which the last ten were lived out in a demanding way at various levels of service to the Church, and everything seemed to be going peacefully—a carpet-bombing occurred inside our marital union.

I will not linger on the particulars, as that would take a whole book, but I will cite some of the damage done. My wife wanted separation at all costs, as she did not feel loved and was determined to start a new life.

Notwithstanding various attempts by everyone from respected priests to our neighbors, absolutely nothing turned her back from her chosen path.

She went to court. Result: I had to leave my home.

Work, in the meantime, started going downhill precisely on account of this stormy situation (I am a salesman); our two sons (17 and 12) became referees of the situation since they could decide at any time which parent to go live with according to their needs or, ultimately, their whims.

Initially they decided to stay at home where they have always lived.

Nothing was left but a pile of rubble!

It has seemed as if God had abandoned us!

Yet this is just what the devil would *like* you to believe!

At this point the situation presented itself as a crossroads. You have to choose to continue taking this ever-narrower uphill path or to turn toward the broader, apparently asphalt one—the road of forgetfulness, and forget everything and everyone, and build a new life (the temptation into which many fall, often stimulated by the world's way of doing things).

Yet a few years before, in Acireale in 1996, I had known Father Renzo Bonetti, national director of the Office of National Pastoral Work, who, with inspired wisdom, managed to impress on me a very important concept: "The sacrament of marriage is not a cove-nant between two, as is commonly thought, but a covenant among three, and it requires at least two to remain intact. The third person composing it is the most important one: Jesus, Who, being a faithful God, never breaks the covenant even when people are unfaithful."

When one of the two spouses breaks the covenant, the faithful spouse, as a minister of the sacrament, may renew his or her 'I do' even without the other spouse, causing the sanctifying grace of the sacrament to be poured out over the other, and to intercede for the other spouse so he or she might be saved.

The way is narrow, bristling with a thousand difficulties, yet it is the path the Lord Himself has blazed; the other is a digression ending in a gorge that the evil one leads us into, away from God's plan. Yet the Lord keeps watch over the path of the one who trusts in Him and wishes to walk according to His precepts..." He who keeps the law preserves himself; and he who trusts in the Lord shall not be put to shame," (Sirach 32:24).

From the moment I was forced to leave my home without a dollar in the bank. The Lord has never allowed me to lack my daily bread. I found another, more satisfying place of work, and after a few days my children came to live with me. Yet the most important thing is that He has placed so much peace in my heart, letting me live in His presence always and in every way through the maternal presence of Mary and through my parish. This very patiently took the place of all those false friends and brothers in the faith who took to hiding as if I had the plague, depriving me of even one word of comfort, which I so needed at that moment. I came to know new brothers from another city that He had sent along my way to give me moral and spiritual support. (Now, I periodically frequent a prayer fraternity in the province of Caltanissetta, which belongs to the Community of Jesus of Turin. See how the Lord manages to weave things together so well?)

Yet the strength I received from the Lord most was daily sharing in the banquet of His Word, of His Body and Blood, offered in the Holy Sacrifice of the Mass, the indispensable nourishment for daily spiritual combat.

I do not know how this situation will end up. I only know God is a merciful Father who has a plan of goodness and happiness for each of His children. It is up to us to decide whether we are on board with this or not.

I wish to conclude with the words of Psalm 26:

> The Lord is my light and my salvation; whom do I fear? The Lord is my life's refuge; of whom am I afraid?
>
> ...One thing I ask of the Lord; this I seek: To dwell in the Lord'S house all the days of my life." (verse 1, 4).

Antonio

God the Father took my hand as a daughter

When, after the separation, I found myself alone, I tried to find other solutions to fill the void inside and out. I did not want to stick with a choice that seemed to me like a jail sentence, an imposition I did not share in making.

So, my first decision was not to remain faithful to the sacrament. Following the counsel of various people, and looking at the environment around me, I started seeking a new companion.

This was the plan I was seeking to realize, yet strangely, I was not calm. I was not able achieve that peace I was seeking. My heart was always unquiet.

Today I testify before God the Father that He has not abandoned me, even when I turned my back on Him. With so much patience and tenderness, sweetly, without forcing me, He took me by the hand. Gradually I began to allow myself to be guided because I was experiencing a liberating love and becoming aware of the great dignity of being His daughter.

These are years in which I remain faithful to the sacrament and prove to my spouse a love which is not that of before, because now I love with God's heart.

Now that I have tasted how good the Lord is, I pray that my spouse allows himself to be taken by His paternal hand as well.

"At your command"

> While the crowd was pressing in on Jesus and listening to the word of God, He was standing by the Sea of Galilee. He saw two boats there alongside the lake; the fishermen had disembarked and were washing their nets. Getting into one of the boats, the one belonging to Simon, He asked him to put out a short distance from the shore. Then He sat down and taught the crowds from the boat. After He had finished

speaking, He said to Simon, "Put out into deep water and lower your nets for a catch." Simon said in reply, "Master, we have worked hard all night and have caught nothing, but at your command I will lower the nets." When they had done this, they caught a great number of fish and their nets were tearing. (Luke 1:1-6)

Lord, I think of that early morning in which You were present near the Sea of Galilee, and of Peter who after a hard night's work on the lake greeted the dawn with empty nets.

I think about his disillusionment, about the weight around the hearts of those with the responsibility of providing for a family and not getting anything from work, just algae and holes in their nets.

I think about Peter gloomily brooding. He moored the boat, glancing furtively at his fishing companions, and then set himself to mending, washing, and fixing the nets. 'Maybe I should get a new job…but what would I do?' While these thoughts crowded around in Peter's mind, his hands moved in the usual gestures, as if mechanically. But then some words waft over, borne by the wind: "Blessed are you…"; "Come to me…"

More than the words, Peter is struck by the tone in which they are spoken, raising his head to see and comprehend, "Ah, it is that Jesus who…"

Back to work, but your eyes keep meeting. You keep working with your head down, but do not feel like chatting anymore, and as you raise your gaze you see Him near you. He gives you a nod that He wants to leave with you on your boat.

Afterward, with that voice which bears you away, He asks you to stop the boat by the shore so He can preach better.

To tell the truth, you wanted to tell Him no, that you are tired after a night of hard work; yet incredibly you are already at the oars, moorings removed and two rowers deftly pushing the boat from the shore. And Jesus is sitting there, returning to teach the crowd.

You, Peter, continue your work and mend the nets but now, next to the Rabbi, you feel His words rising in your heart. Suddenly you no longer feel the bitterness of failure, nor the tiredness of a fisherman's hard work. Even your hands have regained their strength. You are finished in no time, and you dedicate yourself to listening completely. What peace is entering your heart!

After Jesus finishes, He blesses and dismisses the people and you are preparing to bring the boat back to land. You push the oars, but first you look. Jesus, with a look that goes straight to the heart, tells you "*Duc in altum!* Put out into deep water and lower your nets for a catch." You, Peter, begin to tell Him that you tired yourself out in vain for a whole night, yet something within you pushes you to finish the phrase with these words: "…but at Your command I will lower the nets"; and you go.

Lord, I too was on the shore, after a night of wearing myself out for my family, discouraged, ruminating over my failures, and thinking of not going out in my boat anymore. I thought, "Better to pull up dry, take the oars from the oarlocks, and fold up the sail." Yet, You are there, next to me. You have gone out with me in my boat and told me, "*Duc in altum!* Set off!" I am stunned that You wanted me to take off, where the water is deeper, but also clearer.

Now, Lord, I go on your word. I am stretching the muscles of my arms and body to paddle out to sea. But I also want to raise the sail of faith to receive the gusts of Your Spirit and sail on tranquilly because You are at the helm, and I know with You the fishing will be good.

M.P.

Children's Testimony

The Lord rebuilds

This testimony comes from the son of a separated couple who reunited after ten years.

The abandoned wife had prayed ceaselessly for her husband, for his conversion and so that he would return to those duties of a husband and father which he assumed upon marrying.

Supported by faith and hope, this lady has passed through some very difficult trials, and it has produced different fruits: the husband's conversion and return to the home after ten years, the priestly vocation of a son, and welcoming into her own family the child born from her husband's affair.

The whole family is now united and at peace in the love of God.

> These few lines are meant to be a gift of grace for all those children who, like me, have suffered the drama of their parents' separation. They are meant to be a balm on their wounds, provoked by the abandonment of a father or a mother.
>
> Every man and woman who comes into this world bears a vital need written into their DNA: the need for a father and a mother. Animal nature itself teaches this fundamental dependence. We just do not know enough about ourselves fully without a father and a mother! For a child's normal growth the father represents the dear and grave figure who, while offering certitude and security, is also the depository of the lawful order. He is called to remind the children of their proper limits with the end of making them into adults (a child never limited by the father tends to trespass without bounds in his/her experiences, and to grow up with a so called "delirium of omnipotence," the basis of every future childish act). The mother on the other hand is the incarnation of tenderness and affection, of visceral love and compassion.

To ground the life of a boy or girl, to make of them truly men and women, requires the firmness of a father and the tenderness of a mother.

When one assumes the role of the other, or when one of the parents fails in this, insecurity and evasiveness, rage and contempt, can be generated in a child's life.

This was precisely the trial of my own heart in 1989, when my parents' marriage fell to pieces after twenty-seven years.

Everything had seemed "secure" until then, a "given," natural... yet suddenly that order, which had seemed unalterable, changed. Apparently under that veil of security and serenity were hidden fissures and past misunderstandings.

So at age sixteen, an age at which one has greater need of one's parents, I suddenly found myself without a father, who had moved away from home to follow his dreams.

From the depth of my soul there began to rise feelings of insecurity and inferiority. I felt fragile, vulnerable, everything instilled fear in me and a sense of inadequacy. My mother sought to fill this void, but without being able to do so.

I was attending school then and even my studies began to be affected by my suffering. I could not manage to apply myself for even ten minutes without my mind becoming distracted and wandering into thin air. I saw my companions and I felt "dif-ferent," not at the height of what I knew I should be.

That sense of insecurity, which never abandoned me, also led to a psychosomatic development—I felt a deep physical pain in my heart—and for a month I was given medication to calm me down (actually the drugs induced a lot of insomnia).

After this test, I "ordered" myself not to give any more thought to the problem. So, my insecurity now assumed the form of evasion.

I sought evasion in entertainment, to rebuild my self-image with the big men on campus, and to put myself into a stupor with the blaring music of nightclubs. I surrendered myself to the world of appearances, seeking to be what others wanted me to be, to speak and act according to the role models imposed by the advertising industry and the stereotypes acquired from my groups of friends. Gabriel was no more. There was only someone who could please the others, a fascinating mask, which was only the cover over a veil of sadness.

It was obviously an evasion because when I was by myself the pang of loneliness gripped my soul and would not allow me to accept myself for who I was at any deep level. The problem was always there waiting for me, and vanities were my attempts to escape.

Later, meditating on my past and my life experiences, I discovered that behind that evasion was an uncertainty waiting to be filled. Behind every evasion was always an insecurity from which I was fleeing. Behind all the idols man has constructed are always empty spaces to fill. Insecurity is the engine of idolatry, insecurity sets idolatry in motion!

The years passed and the relationship between my father and me grew ever colder. An invitation to dinner or "a couple of hours" spent in a bar did not do it for me.

I continued maturing in my analysis of things and people, and even of what had happened in my family. I went over the first most traumatic stages, and I began to form an opinion which I judged to be "naturally" logical and exact. My father was worthy only of contempt and deserved only my rage.

Following these months of "torment" my father became my antagonist to be killed, the "cause" of my malaise, the "motive" for my being enraged. He was no longer "my father" but someone on whom I could spit up my contempt, the scapegoat to which every sin could be imputed. My rage and my judgment against him were justified on account of "his" errors. He was the one who had been mistaken, while I on the other hand, had undeservedly paid for his mistakes! He was the irresponsible father, I the poor abandoned son!

Similar convictions crowded in on my mind. I fashioned my rope and tightened it, which resulted in an obvious consequence. I no longer loved my father! And, I did not love him anymore because I did not see him with the eyes of a son but those of a merciless judge. During those months, I not only hurt him, but myself, because I could not forgive myself for these brutal feelings. To obey those feelings I had locked myself up into a blind hate. It had become a vicious circle. The more I empathized with my chosen role of victim, the more I felt authorized to despise my father. Every feeling of judgment against him was justified by the conviction of being the victim of his mistakes, and inevitably so. As long as we identify ourselves as the victim of others' mistakes, we will feel entitled to hate and revenge and we will begin to believe murderers rather than acquire greater tenderness and understanding!

Now that my father is back, after ten years away from home, I have discovered that the long period of his return has gone hand in hand with the long and difficult times of my forbearance and compassion towards him. I have discovered that the healing of my heart was as urgent as his own, and that if he had betrayed me as a father, I too—perhaps with even more ferocity—had betrayed him as a son.

Many things have happened over the course of these ten years. The Lord has stooped down to me from above to release me from the death grip I was in. He placed before my wandering steps the figure of a Franciscan friar, who left for heaven just a year ago. In that friar shone the poverty and simplicity of St. Francis. In his eyes glowed the depth—but also the innocence—of God, and from his mouth, like flames of fire, came the severe and sweet words of God for me.

Meeting with that friar three times a week, listening to his thundering and therapeutic words, enjoying his nearness, was the healing touch for a heart restless and thirsting for happiness.

Thanks to him I understood that, as seriously as my parents may have erred, the final word on my destiny and happiness or unhappiness was not theirs, as I was not "just" the product of my father's and mother's mistakes. Because if it truly was that way, then there would be no chance of rescue, there would be no more freedom. Everything without exception would be just the product of whatever others have done to us, just cause and effect and no more freedom.

Even while it is true that a child needs a father and a mother to become a man, my father had about as much right to make a mistake as I did.

Today I am a priest in the Franciscan Order of the Reformed Friars Minor. The unconditional forgiveness I received from God and which I granted my father facilitated and hastened his return to our family.

Even now, there are so many things in my past that I cannot manage to explain to myself, though I still try to find the answers. One of the many is bold, but it comforts me when I consider it. Maybe my father had to err in order for me to learn to seek my true Father, the One in heaven.

St. Francis, when disrobed in the Plaza of St. Rufino in Assisi, returned to his father everything he had, and, without any rebuke against him, pronounced these words, "From now on I will no longer say, "My father Pietro Bernardone," but "Our Father who art in heaven."

It is not from our father and mother that we should find solutions for our insecurity, because inner security is a gift of God and must be sought from Him.

They are not the ones who decide our ultimate happiness or unhappiness. Our parents are only given to us for our sustenance so we can seek a fuller and a higher life, one we cannot receive from them, because the fullness of happiness descends from heaven.

May the Lord grant you peace.

Bro. E.

Riccardo's Pictorial Testimony

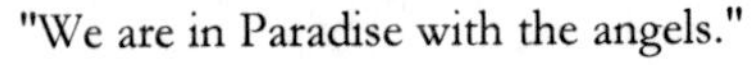

"We are in Paradise with the angels."

Note: Drawing expresses the disire of the little boy Riccardo to see Mommy, Daddy, himself, and his brother together again.

I received only these two testimonials.

I asked other children of separated spouses to express in any manner whatsoever a brief, anonymous testimony, to help children of separated spouses, but they did not feel like doing so.

They have denied what I asked for, directly or indirectly, because evidently it is such a deep and still burning wound that they cannot manage to open up to others about it.

I hope this fact causes everyone to reflect beginning with us spouses, who are directly responsible for these ever-open wounds as well as those persons who, at all levels, try to "help those who are separated." Last, but not least, are those, in the name of a so-called "love," who do not hesitate to break up families, careless of the sufferings and wounds they cause, especially to the children.

So I would like to make, if only on my part, a small gesture, to tell all these innocent suffering children:

> I am sorry, helpless and innocent children, in your parents' name and that of any grownups who have not put you in first place in terms of the choices they have made.
>
> Do not consider yourselves unfortunate, or the children of a distracted God.
>
> Even if your family life is not what it ought to have been, know that it is only in the Lord that everything has meaning, and that He alone can explain it to you, when you ask Him to with your wounded heart.

The Servant of God Francis Paul Gravina

Prince of Palagonia – Palermo 1800-1844

An historical witness of devotion to the sacrament of matrimony is offered to us by the Servant of God Francis Paul Gravina, prince of Palagonìa and of Lercara Freddi, who lived in Palermo in the first half of the 1800's.

> Prince Francis Paul Gravina was born in Palermo on February 5, 1800, the youngest child and only son of Salvatore Gravina and Maria Provvidenza Gravina, princess of Palagonìa and Lercara.
>
> At nineteen years of age, on March 14, 1819, Francis Paul married Nicoletta Filangeri e Pignatelli, one of the "first citizens" of Cutò.
>
> They had no children and, upon discovering the enormous differences which divided them, they lived for a decade ever more spiritually apart. When Nicoletta wound up in an intimate relationship with Francis Paul Notabartolo, the prince of

Sciara, Prince Gravina ended the marriage by sending his wife away. It was 1830.[64]

Given the prince's social position and his immense patrimony, he easily could have found a new companion. Yet following a period of profound crisis, which lasted about a year, he entered the Franciscan Third Order and decided to dedicate his life to the poor.

> …Francis Paul was chaste in that corrupt and hypocritical world which was the high society of the early 1800's. It was a hedonistic culture that cut sexuality loose of all objective moral norms, reducing it to a game of mere consumption, one which today has shed its mask, and which in the Prince's time, though covered beneath a veil of hypocrisy, nevertheless besieged him. The world's suggestions contained the seductive reminder that his great wealth afforded the prince every form of license. His only answer was to enter the Franciscan Third Order and he girded on that white cord of chastity he had brought with him—an invisible one—his entire life, till revealing its existence the day of his death. What many have believed impossible—the perfect observance of chastity—became for him, by the Lord's grace, possible and authentically liberating. His example of chastity, live out in a world enslaved to the senses, offers us a reassuring point of reference.[65]

Francis Paul Gravina took care of the poor of Palermo both in the public forum and even more so in the private view.

He was in charge of the Palermo Friars' treasury and founded a religious congregation, the Daughters of Charity of the Prince of Palagonìa.

---

[64] The informational diocesan Process, *The Initiative, Inventiveness, and Holiness of Francis Paul Gravina, Prince of Palagonìa*, p.13.

[65] U. CASTAGNA, *Amare sino alla fine*, Arte Tipografica Editirice, Napoli, 2001, p.175.

No personal spiritual writings of the prince remain, as he preferred to burn any booklets containing his notes. Still, from some documents and letters, it may be inferred that his spirituality was first to live in obedience to God, day after day.

> ...For Francis Paul, the will of the Father was at the vertex of every manifestation of his concrete and silent love. Regarding the humble servant of God, the only time he opened his soul so it could be read with clarity, he affirmed and echoed the words of the Master in five solemn phrases:
>
> - I declare that I have intended to obey the Supreme Divine Will, manifested in all those circumstances of my life in which Almighty God has placed me.
> - In fact, God has willed to deprive me of children and of any descendants, and in this I recognize the impenetrable decree of the Most High...
> - And how could the Most High better have manifested to me His supreme absolute will that I put aside all pomp of family and perpetuation of my name...?
> - I recognize His sovereign Will, that my patrimony may serve above all things to relieve those who are unhappy and to promote ever more the glory of His divine mercies.
> - Therefore, I follow these high designs of the Divine Will...[66]
>
> He died piously on April 15, 1854. In accordance with his will, his funeral was an example of humility and poverty. Dressed in the Franciscan habit, he wished to be borne in sight of the streets of Palermo with a tile under his head for a pillow.[67]

With his mystical witness, he left a sum destined to have a Holy Mass celebrated every day for the repose of his wife's soul when she died.

---

[66] Ibidem, p.181.

[67] The informational diocesan Process, *The Initiative, Inventiveness, and Holiness of Francis Paul Gravina, Prince of Palagonìa*, p.17.

The widowed Nicoletta later married his friend, had no children, and became such a woman of prayer that her second husband's relatives conserved the princess's prayer book and rosary.

> Loving to the end seemed to have been the fulcrum of the existence of the Servant of God Francis Paul Gravina.[68]

Mystical Witness

Reading from the "Mystical witness of January 21, 1848, in Malaspina, revised, confirmed, and later underwritten with a date of April 1851 in Palermo," declared authentic in every case:

> In the name of the Father, and of the Son, and of the Holy Spirit.
>
> I, the undersigned…Francis son of Paul Ferdinand Gravina prince of Palagonìa, finding myself by God's mercy sound in body and in the full exercise of all my intellectual faculties…
>
> *[Endowment] Number Twelve*: I leave seventy-two *onze* for perpetual endowments, payable from month to month, postponed for alms every two months, i.e., one for my soul from the day of my death, forever and without end, to be celebrated in the chapel of the first department of Mendicant women of the Treasury in Malaspina, where I hope the Sisters of Charity, those good recluses, may wish to combine their prayers to our merciful Lord, so as to take pity on me, as an act of charity.
>
> The other Mass endowment I institute, to be here for long years after the death of my wife, Lady Nicoletta Filangeri, for her soul unto infinity and forever, to be celebrated in the Church of the Holy Agony, this being the only Christian remembrance I can leave.[69]

---

[68] U. CASTAGNA, *Amare sino alla fine*, cit., p.180.

[69] *Last Will and Testament of the Most Excellent Servant of God D.Fr. di Paola Ferdinando Gravina Prince of Palagonía and Lercara*, Fourth edition with additions, Tipografia S. Scibilia, Palermo, 1897.

From this last sentence, it may be deduced that the Prince of Palagonía had remained faithful to the sacrament for 25 years after the separation from his wife.

It is edifying to read in his will this preoccupation of a Christian spouse for the princess Lady Nicoletta Filangeri, whom he continues to call "my wife," to the point of leaving an endowment of Holy Masses to be celebrated, beyond death, on behalf of her soul. We are in the presence of a man who transformed the most painful episode of his married life into a luminous pathway by confiding himself to what he called the "*supreme absolute will of God.*"

Prayer to the Most Holy Trinity

To obtain the glorification of his Servant Francis Paul Gravina

Oh most august Trinity,
By the infinite glory which Jesus
Offers You without ceasing in the Holy Sacrament,
We pray You to glorify Your faithful servant,
Francis Paul Gravina, Prince of Palagonía,
And by his intercession to grant us that grace
Of which we have so much need, and which,
With devoted hearts, we ardently ask of You.

Our Father. Hail Mary. Glory be.

For Italian-language books and information about, as well as images of, the Servant of God the Prince of Palagonía, contact the Superior General of the Sisters of Charity of the Prince of Palagonía, Via Sciuti 102, 90144 Palermo. Telephone 091-343-271; Electronic mail: suoregravina@tiscali.it.

THE SPOUSE IS WITH US

Eucharistic Adoration*

Evening Eucharistic adoration should be presented as a time of repose and of intimate conversation with the Lord.

It is necessary also to take care of the environment: isolated, simple, welcoming, in a small chapel where the Blessed Sacrament can be exposed. Prepare with flowers, light, hymns, and bible passages that can be used to point out the spousal aspect of Christ's presence.

The following suggestions could be used to accompany Eucharistic Service I or II from the *Order for the Solemn Exposition of the Holy Eucharist* (Liturgical Press, Collegeville, MN, 1993), approved for use in the United States of America.

The presiding minister may briefly introduce the celebration, reminding the congregation that the Lord waits on his people to offer them consolation, peace, and love. The Lord already knows all their worries and the difficulties they must confront today. The minister may encourage the congregation to lay down their thoughts and worries at His feet and be silent within and without, allowing the Lord to visit.

---

* (English Publisher's note) The Eucharistic Adoration section in the original Italian edition is modified herein to comply with the norms for the liturgy of the Church as approved for use in the United States.

Appropriate scripture readings may include: Psalm 73 (23-28); Song of Songs (1:7-8; 3:1-4); Isaiah (61:10; 62:1-5, 11); John (6:47-51; 54-58), following the instructions for the Liturgy of the Word given in liturgical books.

A priest or deacon presiding may give a homily, reflecting on Christ the Spouse.

The intercessions on page 79 may be used and adapted as necessary for the needs of the community.

During the period of sacred silence after the homily, there should be prayers, songs, and readings to direct the attention of the faithful to the worship of Christ the Lord.*

Suggested prayers:

Lector: The Lord waits on us to offer us consolation, peace, and love. He already knows all our worries, the difficulties we must confront today. Let us lay down our thoughts and worries at His feet and be silent within and without.

Let us allow the Lord to visit with us.

Lector: Nighttime is a time for waiting, for spousal intimacy, for speaking heart-to-heart. The day is over, we are tired, yet it is precisely for this reason we come to the feet of the Lord to find rest and repose.

Our Lord has prepared what we need. Let us listen to His Word.

---

* (English Publisher's note) from no. 15 "Order for the Solemn Exposition of the Holy Eucharist, Minister's Edition." (Liturgical Press, Collegeville, MN, 1993) citing no. 95 from English Translation of Holy Communion and Worship of the Eucharist Outside Mass, 1974, International Committee on English in the Liturgy, Inc.

Priest: Lord Jesus Christ the Spouse, You alone can satisfy our hunger for love!

All: Grant us to taste of Your Eucharistic banquet!

Priest: Lord Jesus Christ the Spouse, You alone can quench our burning thirst!

All: Grant us Your living water!

Priest: Lord Jesus Christ the Spouse, You alone can comfort and cheer us!

All: Grant us Your healing spousal embrace!

Suggested readings:

Psalm 73 (23-28)

Yet I am always with You;
You take hold of my right hand.

With Your counsel you guide me,
and at the end receive me with honor.

Whom else have I in the heavens?
None beside You delights me on earth.

Though my flesh and my heart fail,
God is the rock of my heart, my portion forever.

But those who are far from You perish;
You destroy those unfaithful to You.

As for me, to be near God is my good,
to make the Lord God my refuge.
I shall declare all Your works
in the gates of daughter Zion.

Song of Songs (1:7-8; 3:1-4)

The following verses may be recited alternating both sides of the chapel or church.

Tell me, you whom my soul loves,
where you shepherd, where you give rest at midday.
Why should I be like one wandering
after the flocks of your companions?

If you do not know,
most beautiful among women,
Follow the tracks of the flock
and pasture your lambs
near the shepherds' tents.

On my bed at night I sought him
whom my soul loves—
I sought him but I did not find him.

"Let me rise then and go about the city,
through the streets and squares;
Let me seek him whom my soul loves."
I sought him but I did not find him.

The watchmen found me,
as they made their rounds in the city:
"Him whom my soul loves—have you seen him?"

Hardly had I left them
when I found him whom my soul loves.
I held him and would not let him go
until I had brought him to my mother's house,
to the chamber of her who conceived me.

Isaiah (61:10; 62:1-5, 11)

I will rejoice heartily in the Lord,
my being exults in my God;
For he has clothed me with garments of salvation,
and wrapped me in a robe of justice,
Like a bridegroom adorned with a diadem,
as a bride adorns herself with her jewels.

For Zion's sake I will not be silent,
for Jerusalem's sake I will not keep still,
Until her vindication shines forth like the dawn
and her salvation like a burning torch.

Nations shall behold your vindication,
and all kings your glory;
You shall be called by a new name
bestowed by the mouth of the Lord.

You shall be a glorious crown in the hand of the Lord,
a royal diadem in the hand of your God.

No more shall you be called "Forsaken,"
nor your land called "Desolate,"
But you shall be called "My Delight is in her,"
and your land "Espoused."
For the Lord delights in you,
and your land shall be espoused.

For as a young man marries a virgin,
your Builder shall marry you;
And as a bridegroom rejoices in his bride
so shall your God rejoice in you.

The Lord has proclaimed
to the ends of the earth:
Say to daughter Zion,

"See, your savior comes!
See, his reward is with him,
his recompense before him."

Matthew (25:2)

"At midnight, there was a cry, 'Behold, the bridegroom! Come out to meet him!

John (6:47-51; 54-58)

Amen, amen, I say to you, whoever believes has eternal life. I am the bread of life. Your ancestors ate the manna in the desert, but they died; this is the bread that comes down from heaven so that one may eat it and not die. I am the living bread that came down from heaven; whoever eats this bread will live forever; and the bread that I will give is my flesh for the life of the world.

Whoever eats My Flesh and drinks My Blood has eternal life, and I will raise him on the last day. For My Flesh is true food, and My Blood is true drink. Whoever eats My Flesh and drinks My Blood remains in Me and I in him. Just as the living Father sent Me and I have life because of the Father, so also the one who feeds on me will have life because of Me. This is the Bread that came down from heaven. Unlike your ancestors who ate and still died, whoever eats this Bread will live forever.

PRAYERS AND THOUGHTS

Prayer for my separated or divorced spouse

(*Communion Notre-Dame de l'Alliance*[*])

Father, I thank You for having given me **N.** as my spouse.

When I was alone, You led me, You offered me Your love. May You be blessed!

I thank You, Lord. When we were both so poor, You united us in Yourself as two diamonds within a single ring. You consecrated us to be one flesh, so as to live the same love which makes You Triune. May You be blessed!

Yet we have been unfaithful to this covenant, and we have been far from You. Betrayed in turn, I have become incapable of true love. Forgive me, Lord. Instead of turning to You, instead of being reconciled in You, we have separated that which You had united; we have broken our family and wounded our children. I beg You, Lord, forgive us!

Yet may You be praised, because You have granted me to understand that all things continue in You, that in spite of our separation, our profound unity remains. And I repeat "I do" every day in response to the grace of the sacrament which unites us in You. Oh yes, Lord, may You be blessed!

---

* (English Publisher's note) *Communion Notre-Dame de l'Alliance* is erected as a private association of the faithful in the Archdiocese of Mechelen-Brussel (Belgium) and the Archdiocese of Rennes (France). The associations are for *Séparés Divorcés Fidéles* married faithful who are separated or divorced.

May You be praised, Father so rich in mercy, for having placed Your forgiveness in my heart toward **N.**

I beg You, allow my spouse to open his/her heart to welcome this forgiveness, and to grant me forgiveness in return. Reconcile us, Lord!

You know how many times I have wounded my spouse, even involuntarily; how my attitude has reopened older wounds.

Humbly, Jesus, I pray You, as You heal my heart, heal that of my spouse as well!

May You be praised, You have granted me Your peace, in the certainty that we will find one another some day.

All the suffering I have endured in this trial I offer You Jesus, so beloved of the Father, for the salvation of our family, for those divided couples, for our separated spouses; for the unity of Your divided Church. In Jesus, through Mary, I bless You my God.

Yes, it is just that I thank You for all that which You have freely given me during these difficult times.

For Your infinite mercy, may You be blessed, Father.

For Your extreme tenderness, may You be blessed, Jesus.

For the fire of Your love, may You be blessed, Holy Spirit.

Through Mary, our Mother, may You be blessed, Lord!

And I bless you, **N.**, my spouse, in the name of the Father, and of the Son, and of the Holy Spirit.

Through the intercession of Mary, our mother, may God, Who is all love, keep you until that day when we will be reunited in Him in eternal glory!

Amen.

Prayer of a Family in Difficulties

Place yourself in God's presence, remembering that a "home," and thus a family, is His doing. Present your own family to Him, along with those of other families experiencing problems.

From Psalm 127

Unless the Lord build the house,
they labor in vain who build.
Unless the Lord guard the city,
in vain does the guard keep watch.
It is vain for you to rise early
and put off your rest at night,
To eat bread earned by hard toil—
all this God gives to His beloved in sleep.
Certainly sons are a gift from the LORD,
the fruit of the womb, a reward.
Like arrows in the hand of a warrior
are the sons born in one's youth.
Blessed is the man who has filled his quiver with them.
He will never be shamed
for he will destroy his foes at the gate.

Ask Mary to help you in this prayer.

From the Gospel according to John, 2:1-10

On the third day there was a wedding in Cana in Galilee, and the mother of Jesus was there. Jesus and His disciples were also invited to the wedding. When the wine ran short, the mother of Jesus said to Him, "They have no wine."

R. Our Father, Hail Mary, Glory be.
Lord Jesus Christ the Spouse, grant us "good wine" as well.
Holy Mary of Cana, pray for us.

Jesus said to her, "Woman, how does your concern affect me? My hour has not yet come." His mother said to the servers, "Do whatever he tells you."

Now there were six stone water jars there for Jewish ceremonial washings,d each holding twenty to thirty gallons. Jesus told them, "Fill the jars with water." So they filled them to the brim. Then he told them, "Draw some out now and take it to the headwaiter." So they took it. And when the headwaiter tasted the water that had become wine, without knowing where it came from (although the servers who had drawn the water knew), the headwaiter called the bridegroom and said to him, "Everyone serves good wine first, and then when people have drunk freely, an inferior one; but you have kept the good wine until now."

R. Our Father, Hail Mary, Glory be.
Lord Jesus Christ the Spouse, grant us "good wine" as well.
Holy Mary of Cana, pray for us.

Prayer for Forgiveness[70]

Lord we now wish to speak with You about the experience of forgiveness.

We all have suffered harm from other people: relatives, friends, people known or unknown.

Lord, You know that often we feel unwelcome, misunderstood, unloved, wounded without even understanding the 'why'

---

70 This prayer may be prayed during Eucharistic adoration. After reading it, everyone may silently listen to all that emerges from memory, without forcing this, and without resisting it. When a painful episode arises, in which we had felt wounded by someone, let us renew our will to forgive and let us ask help of the Lord. If on the other hand we remember having wounded someone ourselves, let us ask the Lord's forgiveness and that this person be healed of the cones-quences of our errors. Let us decide in whatever manner possible, to make amends for this.

for whatever we suffer. Feelings of anger toward others or depression in blaming ourselves have gone back and forth in our minds and our hearts, taking our peace from us.

Yet You, Lord tell us to forgive. You tell us to love our enemies, You exhort us to be merciful as the Father is merciful. And we have sought to forgive, we have even said we are willing to forgive, as long as…

The other says he or she is sorry…

The other changes…

The other admits all his or her faults…

But now, in the light of Your Spirit, we realize this is not true forgiveness, it is *bargaining*, a subtle form of grudge, one that not only prevents us from healing, but which will poison us all the more. You already know this, Lord. The forgiveness we offer is always limited, conditional. You, on the other hand, teach us that forgiveness is to be given always, just as You told Peter: "I tell you not seventy times, but seventy times seven times," always and without conditions.

Lord, we admit to being incapable of forgiving as You wish. Humanly speaking these are offenses which we cannot forgive.

We wish to forgive, but we cannot. It is true, we confess it. We cannot manage to give true forgiveness, forgiveness that removes all resentment.

You alone, Lord, have this ability. You prayed nailed to the cross, "Father, forgive them, they know not what they do." In the very moment we crucified You, You prayed to the Father that we be forgiven.

Just as You Yourself tell us, "Without Me you can do nothing," so in our poverty and powerlessness we turn trustingly to You, and with humility we ask You for the gift of the ability to forgive.

We now approach this path with You in our heart. We wish You to enter into the darkest corners of our existence and to forgive those persons who have wounded us.

Jesus, grant us Your power and surround us with the comforting presence of Your Mother. She, who by a singular privilege of God was preserved from sin, was not preserved from pain. At the foot of the cross, she teaches us the preciousness of our suffering offered to the Father in union with Your own. Amen.

My Hymn for the Day

My life is a flicker, an hour that passes, a moment which soon escapes and is gone. You know, my God, that to love You on earth I have nothing more than today.

I love You, Jesus. My soul tends to You. Be my sweet support; reign within my heart; grant me Your smile, just for a day, just for today.

What does it matter, Lord, if darkness comes over me? No, I cannot ask You for tomorrow. Keep my heart pure, cover me with Your shadow, just for today.

I suffer from my inconstancy; if I think about tomorrow boredom and sadness are born in my heart. What I want, my God, is trial, suffering, and that just for today.

It will do us good to see You soon, upon the eternal shore, oh Divine Pilot, the hand which guides me! Guide my little boat in peace upon the anger of the waves, just for today!

Allow me, Lord, to bury my face in Your neck, where the noise of the world can be silenced. Grant me Your love, preserve me in Your grace, just for today.

Close to Your divine heart, oblivious to whatever may happen, may I no more fear the enemy's shadow, just for today.

Bread of life and of Heaven, Divine Eucharist, oh touching mystery, Who are the fruit of love, come, descend into my heart, Jesus, my pure Host, just for today.

Holy, most sacred vine, deign to unite Yourself to me, and my weak shoot will bear fruit, I will be able to offer You one golden grape cluster, from today on.

I have nothing to offer You as a fruit of love but this fleeting day, this grape cluster in which each grape is a soul. Give me the fire of an apostle, Jesus, and let it be today.

Virgin Immaculate, sweet radiant star of Jesus who unites me to Him, Mother; let me hide under your veil, just for today.

Guardian Angel, cover me with your wing, enlighten my path with your lights. Sweet friend, guide my steps. I call upon you to help me, just for today.

I wish to see Jesus beyond every cloud and veil. Yet, down here, so close to Him ...let His loving face not be hidden from me today.

I wish soon to sing His praises, with no sunset shining upon my soul. Then I will play the angels' harp, I will sing in an eternal today.

St. Therese of the Child Jesus, June 1, 1894
I AM

"I was regretting the past and fearing the future. Suddenly my Lord was speaking:

'My name is I AM.'

He paused.

I waited.

He continued.

'When you live in the past with its mistakes and regrets, it is hard. I am not there. My name is not I WAS.'

'When you live in the future with its problems and fears, it is hard. My name is not I WILL BE.'

'When you live in this moment, it is NOT hard. I am here. My name is I AM.'"

Helen Mallicot

I entrust this book to the Holy Family of Nazareth
That it bear fruit in accordance with God's will,
And I ask the intercession of the Servant of God Francis Paul Gravina
For the peace of spouses undergoing difficulties.

RECOMMENDED READING

The Jerusalem Bible

The Imitation of Christ, Thomas a Kempis

BENEDICT XVI, Encyclical Letter *God is Love*, 2006

Catechism of the Catholic Church, Second Edition, 1994

JOHN PAUL II, Apostolic exhortation *Familiaris consortio*, 1981

JOHN PAUL II, Apostolic letter *Salvifici Doloris*, 1984

JOHN PAUL II, *Mulieris Digntiatem* ("On the Dignity of Women"), 1988

JOHN PAUL II, *Letter to Families*, 1994

JOHN PAUL II, *Letter to Women*, 1995

JOHN PAUL II, Encyclical Letter *Faith and Reason*, 1998

CPSIA information can be obtained
at www.ICGtesting.com
Printed in the USA
FFOW01n2000100418
46224057-47555FF